Write It Forward

■ ■ ■

From Writer to Successful Author

Bob Mayer

First Edition Trade Paperback March 2010

Second Edition, August 2011

Manufactured in the United States

ISBN-13: 9781935712671

Contents

Introduction

"I'm convinced fear is at the root of most bad writing."
Stephen King

What Is Write It Forward?

Publishing is undergoing major changes and these changes are creating new opportunities for writers. *Write It Forward* focuses on educating writers how to be successful authors and help them conquer their fears. *Write It Forward* is a holistic approach encompassing goals, intent, environment, personality, change, courage, communication and leadership that gives the writer a road map to become a successful author in today's rapidly evolving publishing landscape. Many writers become too focused on either the writing or the business end. *Write It Forward* integrates the two putting the control back into the author's hands.

Write It Forward fills a critical gap in the publishing industry paradigm. While there are numerous books and workshops focused on just the writing, this one focuses on the strategies, tactics and mindset a writer needs to develop in order to be a successful author; regardless of the path you choose to publication.

Under the current publishing business model, authors learn by trial and error and networking with other authors. Sometimes it's the blind leading the blind. Given the drastic changes the industry is currently undergoing, the most knowledgeable people admit they have little idea where the industry will be in a year. However, one thing remains constant, writers produce the product and readers consume the product. As we used to say in the Infantry: Lead, follow, or get the hell out of the way. That is a mantra for *Write It Forward*: We must all be leaders.

Authors are the producer of the product in publishing. Agents, editors, publishers, and bookstores are currently the primary contractors, processors, and sellers of that product. On-line retailers also offer an option that didn't exist just a few years ago. While most agents and editors normally get educated in a career path starting at the bottom of an agency/publishing house, writers, from the moment they sign a contract or self-publish their book, are thrust immediately into the role of author as well as promoter. For the new author it's sink or swim. Unfortunately, with the lack of author training, most sink. First novels have a 90% failure rate, which is simply foolhardy. I submit that the success rate for self-publishing is the same as the success rate for getting an agent, publisher, etc. and breaking out. Either way, this book gives you the tools you will need to succeed regardless of the path you take.

The learning curve to become a successful author is a steep one. In the past, the author might have had years to learn, and when needed, re-invent one's self, but the business is now moving at a much faster pace. It's expected that authors not only have to write the books, but also become promoters of their books. Interestingly enough, Promoter (ESTP) is the complete opposite of Author (INFJ) in the Myers-Briggs personality indicator as we will see under **TOOL FOUR: CHARACTER.** It's difficult to go from one mindset to the other. Not only do you have to be Author and Promoter, you must also be Seller (ESJF).

A key aspect of this book is that just by reading it, you prove you are ahead of the pack because you're willing to learn. When I ran a *Write It Forward* workshop in San Diego one participant said that simply getting on the plane to come take the workshop required her to conquer several of her fears.

EXERCISE: In one sentence, write down your goal for reading this book.

Are you able to define it succinctly? Does it have a positive, action verb? An outcome that is clearly visible? We'll be covering all that in **TOOL ONE: WHAT.**

Can You Walk The Line?

Early in the movie *Walk The Line*, Johnny Cash and his two bandmates go for an audition. I recommend watching the movie and focusing on that scene. Here is the dialogue, with my comments in parentheses and bold.

Johnny Cash singing a cover of an old gospel song—within 15 seconds he is halted:
*Producer **(agent)**: Hold on. Hold on. I hate to interrupt... but do you guys got something else? I'm sorry. I can't market gospel **(generic vampire novel, clichéd thriller, whatever)**. No more.*
Johnny Cash: So that's it?
*Producer: I don't record material **(represent a book)** that doesn't sell, Mr. Cash... and gospel **(a book)** like that doesn't sell.*
*Johnny Cash: Was it the gospel or the way I sing it? **(Was it the book or the writing?)***
Producer: Both.
Johnny Cash: Well, what's wrong with the way I sing it?
Producer: I don't believe you.
Johnny Cash: You saying I don't believe in God?
Bandmate: J.R., come on, let's go.
Johnny Cash: No. I want to understand. I mean, we come down here, we play for a minute... and he tells me I don't believe in God.
Producer: We've already heard that song a hundred times... just like that, just like how you sang it.
*Johnny Cash: Well, you didn't let us bring it home **(you didn't get to my hook, climactic scene, whatever)**.*
*Producer: Bring... bring it home? All right, let's bring it home. If you was hit by a truck and you were lying out in that gutter dying... and you had time to sing one song **(write one book)**, huh, one song... people would remember before you're dirt... one song that would let God know what you felt about your time here on earth... one song that would sum you up... you telling me that's the song you'd sing? That same Jimmie*

Davis tune we hear on the radio all day? About your peace within and how it's real and how you're gonna shout it? Or would you sing something different? Something real, something you felt? Because I'm telling you right now... that's the kind of song people want to hear. That's the kind of song that truly saves people. It ain't got nothing to do with believing in God, Mr. Cash. It has to do with believing in yourself.

Johnny Cash: Well, I've got a couple songs I wrote in the Air Force. You got anything against the Air Force?

Producer: No.

Johnny Cash: I do.

Bandmate: J.R., whatever you're about to play... we ain't never heard it.

Within fifteen seconds of singing the song he wrote, the producer knows he is looking at a star.

What Did Johnny Cash Do?

He tried even though the odds of rejection were high. We hear the scary statistics all the time about the slush pile. You can't let that stop you. There are people who won't query because they're afraid of rejection. In essence, they've just rejected themselves. I heard a very weird statistic recently that 90% of people who have a one-on-one with an agent at a conference and are requested to send in their material, never do. There are many reasons for this, but the #1 barrier is fear. Why even do the one-on-one if you are never going to follow through? Your fear has just caused you to reject yourself.

Beyond that, we are witnessing the end of agenting and publishing as it has been known for decades. It's an exciting new world and the author who is willing to put herself out there with courage, has better chances than ever before of succeeding because she controls more of the process of getting the book into the reader's hands.

Johnny Cash walked in the door even though he was afraid. We're going to discuss fear a lot in this book. We're also going to discuss ways you can overcome fears.

He went even though his wife didn't think he had it. There is a scene earlier where he and his band-mates are on the porch playing and Cash's wife storms off and locks herself in the bathroom. She tells him he's wasting his time and he needs to get a *real job*. Some of us have heard the same thing, haven't we?

He stayed after being rejected. Most people think rejection is the end. It's actually a beginning. Use rejection as motivation and as a launching point to try things differently. Rejection is an inevitable part of a writer's life.

He got hit with a double rejection. Not only was he told that the song wasn't good, but his singing wasn't good either. How would you feel if someone told you not only was the book not good, your writing wasn't either?

Even though he was angry, he was respectful. Lashing out, no matter how badly we want to, rarely brings us positive results.

He asked questions. I watch people pitch agents at conferences and many rarely ask questions. They're so focused on pitching they aren't using the time as a valuable learning experience. When Cash asked what was wrong, he got a response that allowed him to focus and change his approach.

He listened. I once got some rejections on a manuscript. Looking back, I remember my agent making a comment two years previously when I was first talking about the idea. I didn't listen carefully enough to what she was really saying, because in retrospect, what every editor said in the rejection letter was what she had said two years ago. We're going to cover communication in **TOOL SEVEN**. Listening for the real message is a key skill successful people have.

He used his **PLATFORM** and tried again. We're always hearing the buzzword Platform. A lot of people feel they don't have one. You do. If you watch the movie, note the look on Cash's face when he's singing the gospel song about his **Peace Within**. He's not peaceful. He's angry. That's his character arc in the movie, finding peace within. So when he finally sings the song he wrote, he's singing an angry song. Because his platform right then is anger: over the death of his brother; the fact his father blamed him for it; and he hated his time in the Air Force, being away from his girlfriend. Basically, he used his real self and mined his emotions. That's your platform.

He conquered his **FEAR**. He not only walked in, he stayed, and he succeeded.

He **CHANGED**. He walked in with one plan, but when it didn't work, he quickly changed that plan.

EXERCISE: Record the one thing you fear the most as a writer?

Here is a very interesting question that writers should ask themselves:

I will do whatever it takes to succeed as a writer, except don't ask me to do . . .

Whatever completes that sentence is your greatest fear as a writer. This question is a great way of finding the one fear that is crippling you. We must attack the ambush, which I will discuss under **COURAGE**.

What is that nagging thing you know you ought to do, but just can't get yourself to do? Is it a craft problem? A business problem? Promotion? Networking? Conquering an addiction? Committing the time to finish your book? Asking for help?

For me, it's rewriting and focusing after the first draft is done. I've always said I've never had an editor or agent come back with a comment on something I wasn't already aware of. Thus, I need to focus and make sure they can't come back with those comments I am aware of. I also have to promote and market better than I have been in the past. As writers, we tend to dislike that part of our job. But it is PART of the job.

EXERCISE THREE: Finish this statement: I'll do whatever it takes to succeed as a writer, just don't ask me to . . .

What Am I Going to Do?

In tough times, it's the tough who succeed. The Green Berets are mentally and emotionally the toughest soldiers in the military. The first thing you'll sense when you meet a Green Beret is that they exude confidence. It's a palpable sensation. They have confidence in themselves, their team, their unit and Special Forces.

How did they become this way?

They **CHANGED**. After all, that's what this is all about. You wouldn't have picked this book up if there wasn't something in your writing life you wanted to change. This book will teach you the path to be able to change and go from writer to author.

There are the nine **TOOLS** in **WHO DARES WINS** and by reading this book you will gain the insight and knowledge to change the same way Special Forces soldiers go from being regular soldiers to being the best. This book gives you a comprehensive plan to build self-confidence so you can conquer fear and succeed as a writer.

The definition of confidence is trust in a person or thing. A feeling of assurance.

Do you want confidence in all aspects of your writing life?

You have goals in your writing life. You want to achieve things. For most of you, the largest obstacle to your success is fear. This book brings you templates and tactics used by the US Army's Green Berets to conquer fear, build confidence and succeed.

But before you start, you have to ask yourself one very important question:

Do you want to change?

It's that simple. Change is extremely difficult, for many different reasons, which will be covered in this book. The good news is, experts have blazed the way for you and you can use their lessons learned and the techniques they developed. I've taught thousands of writers over the last couple of decades and the biggest problem most have is they are not willing to change.

Do you want a life ruled by fear, or do you want to live to the fullest, confident in yourself?

A successful person can make decisions and take action in the face of fear. The successful are head and shoulders above their peers and competition. They accomplish their goals, have pride in themselves, and find a way to achieve what they want in life. The successful writer takes chances and succeeds. The successful writer embraces the changing world of publishing and uses those changes to their advantage.

FEAR is the number one barrier that keeps you rooted in the mundane and ordinary. It is the primary obstacle to achieving your dreams as a writer. Successful people take action despite their fears. As you'll discover as you read, it is not a question of ignoring fear, but rather the opposite: you must factor fear into your writing life and deal with it.

A lot of what you will learn in this book seems common sense. Some will also be counter-intuitive. We make repeated mistakes without learning from them. This book teaches you how to focus, learn from errors, and not repeat them. Since we all make mistakes, the positive news is that correspondingly there are ways we can improve. We are emotional creatures, and most often our emotions overrule our common sense. Intellectually, our subconscious overpowers our conscious. So we will focus on trying to find the real reasons why we do things, which are often right in front of us, but we are blind to. We will spend quite a bit of time trying to determine blind spots, which are often the roots of our fears.

A lot of what is covered is using my experience as an example. I'm going to give you snippets from my writing career—what worked, what didn't work. From this you will see how I learned all this material. Hopefully, you won't make the same mistakes I did. One advantage is that I have experience in both traditional and non-traditional publishing. My first novel came out in 1991 and I have had over 40 books traditionally published since then. In 2010 I formed Who Dares Wins Publishing with Jen Talty and we now have over 30 books published and have gained considerable experience concerning eBooks, Print-On-Demand and non-traditional publishing. The future of publishing is not going to be a straight and narrow path, but rather a byzantine winding trail with as many opportunities as there are dangers.

This book will show you how to use the strategic tools. Strategic is the big picture. For example, in **TOOL ONE**, we're going to talk about your single strategic goal as a writer. You will have one strategic goal, stated in one sentence, with an active verb.

This book will show you how to use the supporting tools. Supporting is everything that falls under strategic. You have to align everything you do tactically in order to achieve your strategic goals.

Write It Forward is broken down into three areas from the title of the book *Who Dares Wins: The Green Beret Way To Conquer Fear And Succeed* (Pocket 2009), with three steps in each, that I managed to get down to one word each (even beginning with the same letter in each area):

Overview of the *Write It Forward* Program and The Circle of Success

AREA ONE: WINS
TOOL ONE: WHAT specifically do you want to achieve with your writing?

TOOL TWO: WHY do you want to achieve these particular goals?

TOOL THREE: WHERE will sustained change occur?

AREA TWO: WHO
TOOL FOUR: Understand ***CHARACTER.***

TOOL FIVE: What is ***CHANGE,*** and how do you accomplish it?

TOOL SIX: How do you build the ***COURAGE*** to change?

AREA THREE: DARES

TOOL SEVEN: COMMUNICATE your change to the world.

TOOL EIGHT: Take **COMMAND** of your change.

TOOL NINE: COMPLETE the Circle of Success and change.

Why Use Write It Forward?

It's the difference between ordinary and elite. Elite is a word that has a bad rap. It simply means a group of people considered to be the best. To get published, you've got to be the best in that slush pile. You have to be the best among the masses who are self-publishing. Ordinary doesn't cut it in publishing.

Success is a struggle. I recently read a book by Barbara Ehren-reich titled: *Bright-sided: How the Relentless Promotion of Positive Thinking Has Undermined America*. Yes, I am not a fan of '*The Secret*'. You have to do more than just think your way into success. You must take action. However, as you will see under **TOOL FIVE: CHANGE**, the first step of change is thinking differently. But by itself, that is not change.

The *enemy* is closer than we think. I have always been my own worst enemy. No one else writes my books. I do. I can complain as much as I want about agents, publishers, editors, the reading public, but I own my writing, my book and my career. The only one who can stop me, is me.

Do you do things the *right* way or the *brave* way? Near the end, we're going to talk about breaking rules. We used to say in Special Forces: If you ain't cheating, you ain't trying. We'll discuss the para-doxical three rules of rule breaking.

You have to go from being a craftsman to an artist. You have to master the craft in order to become the artist. You have to learn the rules before you start breaking them.

Write It Forward causes you to focus, to ask why. When I critique, I always ask, "why did you do that?" Because there are no strict rules of writing, you can do anything. But you should consciously know **WHY** you are doing it and have a good reason.

It takes you out of crisis management into management. Suc-cessful people act, not react. One thing I learned in my writing career was that I was reacting too much: once you have a multiple book contract, you're reacting to that contract. That's okay, but don't stay in that mode forever. To break out, you have to act. To make the decision to go from traditional publishing to indie publishing, I had to act decisively.

I've used, taught, and lived this. From West Point, through the Infantry, Special Forces A-Team leader, teacher at the JFK Center at Ft. Bragg, my writing and teaching career, my consulting business, my publishing company—this is pulling it all together.

IT WORKS. Special Forces are the most elite soldiers in the world. A lot of what I'm presenting here is what they learned from centuries of 'blood' lessons. Also, I'm presenting things I've learned from successful authors such as Susan Wiggs, Elizabeth George, Terry Brooks, Jenny Crusie, and many others.

"I am always doing that which I cannot do in order to learn how to do it." Pablo Picasso.

A successful writer is a confident writer. Look at the differences between a confident person and one with low confidence:

LOW CONFIDENCE	HIGH CONFIDENCE
Hiding/Ignoring mistakes	Admitting mistakes & learning from them
Doing what others think you should	Doing what you know is right
Letting fear dictate your actions	Using courage to overcome your fear
Staying in status quo (misery)	Taking risks & changing, despite difficulty
Letting others take charge	Taking charge
Letting each day happen	Having goals, plan, and on a path everyday

"In war, everything is simple, but even the simple is difficult."
Carl Von Clausewitz

Please remember, everything I say is simply my opinion. There are no absolutes. One tenet of *Write It Forward*, though, is: Anything that you read in this book that makes you angry or upset is the thing you have to focus on. Our greatest defenses are built around our greatest weaknesses. Anger is an indicator of a need to change.

EXERCISE: Record the one thing that motivates you the most as a writer.

Most successful people use elements of *Write It Forward*, they just call it different things. Nora Roberts, the #1 selling writer in the world, sells 27 books every minute. She has 182 books in print. She says that, "you're going to be unemployed if you really think you just have to sit around and wait for the muse to land on your shoulder."

Ever watch Chef Ramsay? *Kitchen Nightmares*? He would be called in to assist restaurants that were failing (BTW new restaurants have the same failure rate as new novelists: 90%). His flow of evaluating and helping the restaurant reminds me a lot of my *Write It Forward* concept. To start, he would walk in, sit at a table, look at the menu and order a meal.

The menu tells him the focus of the restaurant. Often, there is too much stuff on it. He tells the owner and chef: pick one meal that's going to be your moneymaker. Don't try to do too much. Many authors use the large menu technique when approaching an agent or self-publishing: I've got a paranormal romance, a thriller, a YA book—which do you want?

Cherry Adair said a smart thing at the Emerald City Writers Conference in her workshop. You can write in multiple genres, but if you want a career in publishing, pick *one* genre and become very good at it. *Then* you can write the other stuff. I've written military thrillers, romance, suspense, science fiction, non-fiction, paranormal romance, and a bunch of other stuff. I wish I had heard Cherry's advice 20 years ago.

As a writer, there are times you have to close doors. I sold back the third book of a three-book deal to the publisher because I knew, based on the sales numbers from the first book that the third would just die. I didn't want to write a book that would die. I wanted to spend that time writing a spec book that had a better chance at success. Walking away from a contracted book is a hard door closing, but a necessary one.

When I began thinking about Who Dares Wins Publishing, I had to sit down and figure out what exactly my specific niche was going to be and stick to it. The tendency is to want to expand, to cover a lot. Strangely, in the age of the Internet, people's views are becoming narrower, not broader. You have to become known as *THE* person who does *THAT* thing. Be *THE* writer of *THAT* type of book.

Chef Ramsay then eats the meal. It tells him the quality of the food and how good the chef is. How good is your writing? The best idea in the world has to be supported by solid writing.

A big problem he runs into time and time again is that no one is clearly in charge in the restaurant. No matter how good your agent, editor, publisher, etc. are, you are in sole command of your writing career.

Often the problem is the chef. But the owner is afraid to fire the chef. I've let go of four agents. I did it *before* I went looking for a new agent. It's hard. It's scary. But it is something you control. I also made the decision to switch from traditional publishing to indie publishing. To do that, I had to turn from the business that had supported me for 20 years. A key thing to remember as a writer is pretty much the only power you have in the publishing business is the power to say NO. Close a door.

Ramsay goes back to the restaurant several months later to see how they are doing. What's amazing is often the restaurant is out of business, or still teetering on the edge of failure because they have not implemented his recommendations even though they asked for his help.

Change is hard. In **TOOL FIVE** of *Write It Forward*, we discuss the 5% rule. When I taught for Writers Digest I found that 95% of the students who had paid good money for the course, changed very little.

They re-arranged deck chairs on the Titanic. (BTW, when I saw that movie, the young girls in the row behind us didn't know the ship was going to sink. They were quite horrified when it did.)

I think Chef Ramsay and Kitchen Nightmares set a good example for author nightmares. Change or be left behind.

I was watching a special on the band Coldplay. They talked about how they have a list of rules they post in the recording studio when they go in to cut a new album. One would think a rock band would be carefree and creative and all that other black beret, smoking cigarettes on the corner, poet-stuff. Nope. They said they learned to make those rules the hard way and they absolutely stick by them. It is the only way they can channel their creative energy into a quality product. In Special Forces we call that Standing Operating Procedures. Under **TOOL SEVEN**, I discuss why you need SOPs as a writer.

The one character trait I have found that successful writers have in common, over and over again, is the ability to consistently work hard.

About Bob Mayer

To start off every workshop I give with a brief background of myself. I believe it's important for you, the reader, to have a better understanding of who I am and why you should listen to me. Think about it. I'm a fiction writer. I make my living making things up.

But I'm not going to tell made-up stories to you here in *Write It Forward*. I've made my living writing for the last twenty something years. I've been published by the Big Six in New York City, had four different agents and written in at least four different genres. Now I am self-publishing my backlist and I'm CEO of my own company, Who Dares Wins Publishing. I've been able to sustain a career in a crazy industry because I've been willing to learn and adapt. *Write It Forward* is about YOU the author becoming successful in a business where 95% of people who even manage to get published or self-publish fail.

The person stopping you is you.

Understand that everything in this book is filtered through my point of view. Through my experiences in life as a Green Beret, a NY Times Best-Selling Author and as a publisher. How you interpret what is in this book is filtered through your unique experiences in your own life.

Here is a brief bio.

I am a best-selling author of over 50 books. I am a West Point graduate, served in the Infantry and Special Forces (Green Berets): led an Infantry platoon and then Battalion and Brigade level Reconnaissance platoons; commanded an A-Team and as a Special Forces battalion operations officer; commanded a training company, and was an instructor/writer at the JFK Special Warfare Center & School at Fort Bragg. I also served in Special Operations Western Command on a variety of classified assignments. I have been studying, practicing and teaching change, team-building, leadership and communication for over thirty years. I created my own publishing company Who Dares Wins Publishing with Jen Talty.

WHO DARES WINS: The Green Beret Way To Conquer Fear And Succeed was published by Simon & Schuster. **WHO DARES WINS** is an excellent program for small businesses and teams to learn how to become elite like the Green Beret A-Team. I used the same concept for *Write It Forward: From Writer To Successful Author* to help writers utilize the **WHO DARES WINS** concepts.

My books have hit the NY Times, Wall Street Journal, Publishers Weekly, USA Today and other best-seller lists. I have been published in many genres, including thriller, science fiction, suspense, romance and non-fiction. I have appeared on PBS, NPR, SyFy, and the Discovery Channel and in USA Today, The Wall Street Journal, Sports Illustrated, Forbes, International Business Times, and Army Times among other publications as an expert consultant. I have sold millions of books around the world.

I am an honor graduate of the Special Forces Qualification Course, the Special Warfare Center Instructor Training Course and the Danish Royal Navy Fromandkorpset School. I am Master Parachutist/Jumpmaster Qualified and earned a Black Belt while living in the Orient and also taught martial arts. I earned an MA in Education. I also graduated the International Mountain Climbing School and completed 14 marathons including qualifying for the Boston Marathon and running it three times.

I've spoken before and worked with over 1,000 groups and organizations, ranging from SWAT teams, the University of Georgia, IT teams in Silicon Valley, the CIA, Fortune 500 companies, numerous small businesses, Romance Writers of America and the Maui Writers Conference. I have written a Staff Walk for the Gettysburg Battle for the Special Warfare Center; a Special Forces Forward Operating Base Standing Operating Procedure; a Special Forces A-Team Standing Operating Procedure and contributed to the Special Forces Maritime Operations Standing Operating Procedure. I am an adjunct faculty at the University of Washington teaching communication.

I bring a unique blend of practical Special Operations Strategies and Tactics and mixed it with the vision of an artist to create a program to help you overcome fear and succeed.

Now that you know a little bit about me, lets get started on the road to being a successful author.

"Creativity without strategy, or strategy without creativity, is unlikely to get either parties the results they are anticipating." Lincoln Davies.

Area One: Wins

What Do You Want To Achieve With Your Writing?

We'll cover **WINS** first, because it's best to have a clear direction as you work through the next two areas. Using *Write It Forward* techniques in this area, you begin by specifying goals, then understanding why you want to achieve them, and finish with studying the situation in which you are trying to have success.

We will work on **WHAT** (goals) you want to achieve. Then examine **WHY** (intent) you want to achieve your goals. Then study the **WHERE** (environment) change will occur.

Goals are future oriented. Planning for the future is a cornerstone of Special Forces. A successful individual acts, while the norm is trying to maintain the status quo with your environment. Most people do not have well-defined, clear goals and thus never change. They spend significant time and energy in their lives reacting, instead of acting. Trying to achieve a goal through reaction is a self-defeating approach: you're allowing your efforts to be dictated by external forces and others' goals. To avoid this, it's important that you apply the three tools in this area to your writing, and then you'll be on the path to succeed the *Write It Forward Way*.

When I run workshops, I find that less than 10% of the writers have a clear idea of where they want to be in five years with their writing career. Most are simply too focused on writing that first manuscript and trying to sell it; or if published, selling the next manuscript and staying alive in the business. You need to be striving to succeed, not striving to survive.

Goals Overview
- *You must have goals that are clearly defined and can be stated in one sentence.*
- *You must understand why you're trying to achieve your goals, what impact they'll have on your environment, and how your environment affects you.*

Overall Goal Problems
- *Writers don't have a career goal.*
- *Writers don't clearly understand what they want to achieve with their writing.*
- *Writers don't clearly understand what they want to achieve with their book.*
- *The writer is working in conflict with her own environment and the publishing world.*

Goals
- *Goals are future oriented.*
- *The normal writer spends his time and energy reacting.*
- *The successful writer spends his time and energy acting.*

Tool One: What

Clearly understanding your goals keeps you on target to succeed. As Casey Stengel said: *"If you don't know where you're going, you're liable to end up somewhere else."*

Everything we cover in *Write It Forward* works both ways: For you and for your book. So you need to know both your goals and your book's goals.

The problem many face is that most unpublished writers are desperate to just be published. Once published, they're desperate to sell the next book. Then the next. Thus, most writers don't have a strategic goal.

Before we get into the details of goals, though, let's discuss where success comes from. Is it talent? Or is it perseverance? We used to argue this all the time at the Maui Writers Retreat/Conference among the faculty.

There is a word that applies to this question: *GRIT.*

Science has too long focused on intelligence & talent as determiners of success. And it's not. *The key to success is to set a specific long-term goal and to do whatever it takes until the goal has been achieved.* That's called **GRIT** (defined as courage and resolve; strength of character).

Duckworth did a study in 2008 at West Point. **GRIT** was the determining factor of Beast Barracks success. My plebe squad had five members. Three of them didn't make it to Christmas the first year. They weren't bad people; they just didn't really WANT it. It's the same in Special Forces training. There are those who go into it because they want to wear a green beret. They don't make it. The ones who make it want to BE a green beret. There are those who want the lifestyle of 'author'. They never get published. The ones who want to BE an author make it.

Way back in 1869, Stephen Jay Galton wrote a book titled: *Hereditary Genius*. He found that *ability combined with zeal & capacity for hard work* trumps talent.

Woody Allen says "80% of success is showing up." Again and again.

Do You Have A Fixed Mindset Or A Growth Mindset?

Successful people have a growth mindset. The problem with many *talented* people is that they know they are talented; they think that they already know everything they need to know. So they never adapt and change and grow. A growth mindset person believes they can always learn more. Successful authors are always expanding their craft and their business savvy, especially in today's rapidly changing publishing environment.

Strategic And Supporting Goals

The Hierarchy Of Goals
- *Overall Writing Goal. (Strategic)*
- *Book goal. (Supporting)*
- *Business goal (Supporting)*
- *Shorter range/daily goals (Supporting)*

So let's talk about your strategic writing goal. It can be anything, but it's important that you lock it down. Some broad examples:
- *I will be a NY Times best-selling thriller author in five years.*
- *I will write my memoir for my grandchildren in the next three months.*
- *I write part-time simply because it is a hobby and spend an hour a day on it.*

- *I want to be published within 2 years by a major, traditional press.*
- *I will have my book in print within 2 months via self-publishing.*
- *I will earn X amount of dollars per month indie publishing in six months.*
- *I will write a book that will help people with —— and spend the next three years using it to bolster and complement my speaking career.*

The Importance Of Your Strategic Goal

It starts your creative and practical process. Everything you do is going to be slanted to support this goal. Your strategic goal determines your supporting goals. Writing it down and posting it where you can see it every single day helps keep you focused. It determines how you approach the publishing business. It is also the core of your work regime. It is the core of your marketing campaign.

All supporting goals must align with it in the hierarchy.

Supporting Goals

The key to exactly knowing your strategic goal is that every supporting goal that follows is designed to support it. Thus, everyone's path will be different based on having different strategic goals. Everything that you are getting in this book is filtered through your specific strategic goal. When you go to a writers' conference, everything you hear is also filtered through your strategic goal. So two people attending the same session are going to walk out with two different impressions, each filtered through their point of view, which is shaped by their strategic goal.

What I have seen—and experienced—is that most writers do their first book blindly and don't have a plan beyond finishing it and trying to sell it. Most writers spend too much time and effort trying to sell their first book, rather than moving on to a second and third manuscript. Rarely does a first manuscript sell. The most important thing you must do once you complete your first book is start writing your second.

Most published authors I know sold somewhere around manuscript number two or three. At a daily level, many writers don't have a plan for writing every day.

When you state your goals, they should be done in *one sentence.* The sentence should have a positive verb that indicates the action you want to use to achieve your goal. The verb must indicate an action you control—to an extent. In publishing, you control the writing and the way you approach the business. Beyond that, the publishing gods are fickle. "I will become a NY Times Bestselling author in five years" seems a bit lofty. But here's the bottom line: if that's what you want to achieve, then state it. And then develop a plan to do it. This greatly increases your odds of achieving the goal than the hit-or-miss method. I've listened to many successful people and many of them set out with lofty goals, and then busted their butt to achieve those goals. As you will see shortly, once you have that strategic goal, it changes everything you do, because everything you do has to support that goal. Remember, if you don't set that high goal, you are pretty much guaranteed to never achieve it.

Your goal should have an external, visible outcome. Just as in your novel your character's goal should be something concrete and external, so should yours. This is important because otherwise how will you know when you have achieved it? Being successful is a great goal, but how do you define success? There's a large difference between striving to survive (which most people are doing) and striving to succeed.

You should have a time lock for achieving the goal, unless time is of no consequence to you. For most of us, time is the most valuable asset we have. A time lock also keeps us focused and working toward a specific objective in a specific amount of time.

Why Post Goals

Posting goals make them real. Writing anything down takes it from the vagaries of our brains (very dangerous place) to the real world.

When I used an example of a strategic goal of *NY Times best-selling author in five years*, you also have to remember the caveat I put in the introduction. Everything in this information is being channeled through my experiences. My first book was published in 1991. I've had over 40 published since then with a variety of publishers in a variety of genres. Some of those books have hit the best-seller lists. Some have bombed. Same writer, different publishing experience. Susan Wiggs' first book came out in 1988. She hit the NYT extended list about 5-6 years ago. She hit #1 this year. She points out that the same plan failed with two publishers before she got her current one. The key thing, though, is that she kept pursuing her goal and didn't quit.

It's great to have the lofty goal. But also understand it's going to take time. I see people getting frustrated that they had set goals and not achieved them. Maybe you weren't as focused then as you are now? Maybe you were setting goals in a fog, not quite sure of the path? That's one of the reasons I wrote this book, to clear away the fog, so you can stay on a true path.

I've been watching the latest trends via social media (Twitter, blogs, etc.) but I still think publishing is essentially the same, whether you go traditional or self: write a good book, start writing your next book, get published or self-publish, market, and word of mouth makes or breaks you. We'll discuss marketing and some of those things you should do later in this book.

Keep It Positive-A Negative Goal Accepts Defeat

Here's another thing about stating your goal. Putting it out there, verbally and in writing, is a form of making a commitment. I know many writers get some static from those around them about all the time and money they invest in writing when they are unpublished and there seems to be no payback. If all those around you see is you sitting in front of a computer staring into space and then going off to conferences, they might start to question what you are doing. Letting others know your goal is committing you to trying to achieve it and also lets others know you're serious about what you are trying to achieve. Then showing your supporting goals such as how much time you allocate each day to writing, attending conferences, taking workshops, etc. will make sense in terms of the framework of the larger, long-term goal.

It also puts pressure on you to stick to your goals. I know many people who are afraid to clearly state their goals because by not doing so, they can slack off day after day. Also, some are afraid to state goals because they fear ridicule.

In 1987 Jim Carrey was 25 years old and a struggling comic. He drove his Toyota up Mulholland Drive in LA. Overlooking the city he wrote himself a check for $10 million. He dated it 1995 and noted it was *for acting services rendered.*

He was wrong. In 1995, his price for a movie was $20 million.

Things To Consider When Trying To Figure Out Your Goal

Did anyone else achieve this goal (write this kind of book; have this type of career)? You are not the first one trying to achieve the goal. When I asked Susan Wiggs for career advice the first thing she said she did was study authors who had achieved what she wanted. She cited Nora Roberts and Suzanne Brockman among others. Was that shooting high? Yes. Did she do it? She is now a #1 New York Times best-selling author.

What do you fear doing? I have often found that many writers are afraid of writing about the things closest to them. Which means they are afraid to write their passion. Why didn't Johnny Cash walk in and sing his own song right from the start? I submit that he was afraid that his own music wasn't good enough. More importantly, and dangerous, it was too close to some raw emotions boiling inside of him. But when he sang a song close to his heart and passion, it connected with listeners.

Questions To Ask To Get To One Sentence
- *What do I want to do?*
- *Why do I want to do it?*
- *Why should anyone else want to do it? (History & Research)*

- *What is the most important thing I want to achieve?*
- *How will I know when I have achieved my goal? What will have happened?*
- *(The one sentence is the **What**, not the **How**.)*
- *How have others defined it?*
- *How long did it take others to achieve this goal?*

What was your original goal when you began writing? The good news is you had one. The bad news is you might well have forgotten it. That original goal is key. It is usually the spark of inspiration. It is the foundation of you as a writer, the seed, from which all else comes. It is your Strategic Original Idea.

EXERCISE: What is your strategic goal as a writer?

One question I do hear a lot from writers regarding the *Strategic Goal* is what if the goal seems unrealistic? A dream? Not reality? No strategic goal is a fantasy unless you say it is. That is a subconscious negative. If you want to be a NY Times best-seller, then put it out there. If you want to earn $20,000 a month as an indie author, state it and then go for it. Own it. You will never achieve any goal unless you set it. So aim high.

One of the things I do at Who Dares Wins Publishing is email my business partner Jen Talty with a sales goal for the next month, the next 6 months and for the end of the year. One of our goals is to sell a million eBooks and we set that goal back when we were selling 347 eBooks a month. Now we are selling 65,000 eBooks a month (June 2011) and have been increasing every week. We are getting closer to our goal because we put it out there, owned it, and then set up the supporting goals of how to get there.

Key Supporting Goal—*WHAT* To Write

At the core of being a writer is the writing. Everything else is secondary to that. So this is the most critical supporting goal you need to define.

Mark Twain said, "write what you know." This makes sense. Your platform is based on your experiences. However, there is a danger to this as you might be too close to reality and not be able to achieve the suspension of disbelief that fiction requires.

What is your platform? What unique experiences have you had in your life? What could your publisher put on the back inside flap of your hardcover that would make readers think you knew something about what you are writing?

Write what you want to know. My friend Elizabeth George writes literary British mysteries. She was a schoolteacher in Orange County, CA. But she traveled to England and became fascinated with it, particularly the class structure. So she invented two characters, one a handsome rich nobleman, the other a plain, lower class woman and teamed them together as detectives.

Write what you are passionate about. Study writers. Some writers focus on a specific locale that they are passionate about: Dennis Lehane and Boston; Michael Connelly and LA. Others a specific topic: Stephen Pressfield and ancient battles. Others a specific character: Sue Grafton and Kinsey Milhone.

Write to fulfill a need. Sometimes you just have to say something. Be careful, though. Make sure you aren't lecturing the reader. The primary reason people read fiction is for entertainment. So what makes a consumer want to read it? How does your story connect emotionally with the reader?

"If you do not tell the truth about yourself, you cannot tell it about other people." Virginia Woolf.

This is a **FEAR** many writers have. They feel they are revealing too much of themselves in their writing and exposing themselves to the world.

You are.

But don't sweat it. How many authors would you recognize if you saw them?

And even if you put your mother in the book as a character, it's probably not a problem because:

- *You have to write the book.*
- *You have to sell the book.*
- *Your mother has to read the book.*
- *Your mother has to recognize herself in the book. Most won't.*

People are going to know things about you from what you write. You can't let that inhibit you. Remember, you always have the excuse it's fiction. I start many of my presentations by reminding people I'm a professional liar. I get paid to make things up.

No matter what, once you are published, someone is not going to like what you wrote. And they will feel it's their solemn duty to let you know that. It's part of the job.

Out of every 100 emails I get about my books, 99 are nice. That 1 that isn't used to really bum me out until I adjusted my attitude. Now I do the following:

If it's a nasty email (not a thoughtful critical one), I immediately stop reading and hit delete. I don't need to pollute my mind with such thoughts. Then I smile and think, *that book really must have affected that person to get them so angry*. I'd rather have anger, than apathy.

A question that always comes up at conferences is: "What's hot?" The answer: Who cares?

I'm not saying you should ignore the market. Indeed, you have to study and follow the market, because it's the business and it's important to profile your readers so you know how to best reach them when your book is published. However, there is such a time-lag in publishing that what's hot now, might not be hot three years from now (year to write book, year to sell it, year in production).

That timeline is changing, but so far, not that much for traditional publishers. For self-publishers, we can have a book up in a day on electronic platforms. But I doubt you can write a book in a day based on what's hot.

Writing about something you don't care about, but are doing it simply to try to ride the latest vampire/steampunk/lawyer/serial killer wave, will show up in the writing.

You don't control the market. Sometimes you hit things at the right times, sometimes you aren't lucky. I wrote a suspense novel (*Body-guard of Lies*) with two female leads: one an assassin, the other a housewife. I received little interest in it during the 90s. Now female leads in a thriller are hot.

My vampire book (*Area 51 Nosferatu*) came out before vampires were hot.

I recently wrote historical fiction with the first book covering 1840 until the battle of Shiloh in the Civil War (*DUTY, HONOR, COUNTRY, a Novel of West Point & the Civil War*). I was working on it for a while before someone pointed out to me that 2011 is the 150th Anniversary of the start of the Civil War. That was just a coincidence. I wrote that book because I'm passionate about the subject matter and the people involved.

Key Supporting Goal—How Do You Approach The Publishing Business?

- *Once you know what your strategic goal is and what you want to write, you have to decide what type of publishing medium will support that goal*
- *Do you want a major, traditional publisher*
- *Do you want to self-publish*
- *Do you want to vanity publish*
- *Do you want a regional, prestige publisher*
- *Do you want to go e-book and POD*
- *The key is which medium will support the strategic goal*

Making The Leap From Supporting To Strategic

The strategic is an objective. To get to the objective you have to do something every day. Keep an excel spreadsheet that lists what word count you will do each day. As the days go by you can look at it and see your progress.

One thing I write about in Who Dares Wins is not only keeping a *to do* list, but also a *done* list. You have to see what you've accomplished in order to keep going.

Another thing I do with my work in progress is print it out every fifty pages or so and put it in three ring binder. Then get away from the computer with my red pen. It looks different on paper. But also, having those pages in hands gives me a sense of accomplishment.

The Hierarchy Of Goals Example

Here I'm going to show you how this would work for an author.

Strategic Goal

- *I will be a New York Times best-selling author within five years*

Supporting Goal (Book)

- *I will write a unique thriller, in the vein of James Rollins, but different because of ????, in the next six months*
- *I will be researching and outlining the second book in the series*
- *I will research and come up with the idea for the third book in the series*

Supporting Goal (Business)

- *My thriller will be the first of three similar thrillers featuring the same protagonist, an ex-Navy SEAL, Harvard educated, anthropologist with one arm who secretly cross-dresses. (You might laugh at that last part, but a big key to making your book different from everyone else's is having a unique protagonist with an anomaly that makes them stand out from all the other protagonists)*

- *Every week I will research and make a list of five agents interested in this genre*
- *I will attend a writers' conference this month where there is an author who has what I want and attend every session I can. I will not stalk her, but I will try to talk socially to her given the opportunity, which I will make by NOT hiding in my room, but spending every available minute in workshops and in the conference area*
- *I will attend a writers' conference in four months where there will be agents that represent my type of novel to get feedback from them. Ditto for the stalking*
- *I will follow the publishing business to see what the trends are*

Supporting Goal (Shorter Range)
- *This is essentially how you organize your monthly, weekly, and day to day writing*
- *I will get up an hour earlier every day to write*
- *I will stay up an hour later every night to write*
- *I will write five pages a day. Every day*
- *I will bump my Kindleboard threads every 7 days*
- *I will spend 20 minutes twice a day on Twitter*
- *I will blog twice a week, on Tuesday and Friday. Every week*
- *I will have a draft done in ten weeks*
- *I will rewrite the draft for plot, for character, for symbols, for subplots*
- *As I rewrite, I will write my query letter and synopsis*
- *I will continue to rewrite my query letter and synopsis until they are the best I can make them*

The Hierarchy Of Goals Must Be Aligned
This is your responsibility, not your agent's or editor's. If goals are not aligned, there is inherent conflict and wasted time and energy. Awareness and honesty are key. You have to truly evaluate what you want to do, and how far you are willing to go in order to achieve your goals.

You have ONE strategic goal as a writer. However, that doesn't mean you have to be working on only one thing. In fact, as you'll see later when we discuss **Catastrophe Planning**, you probably should be working on more than one thing. The key each day is to remember where your primary focus is.

Also, quality is better than quantity. That's a maxim of *Write It Forward*, because it's a maxim of Special Forces. The number one marketing tool for a writer is to have a good book.

So when I watch something like #nanowrimo or #writegoal on twitter, I think it's good that people are on task and producing, but am also concerned about the quality of the material.

I can't write more than one piece of fiction at a time. I can't cross the creative wires. However, I am very prolific because my work schedule looks like this on any given day:

- *Priority #1:* My fiction work in progress
- *Priority #2:* My non-fiction work in progress. I find writing non-fiction very different than fiction. So the wires don't cross
- *Priority #3:* Working on getting Who Dares Wins Publishing continuing to expand
- *Priority #4:* Working on new concepts for fiction and non-fiction
- *Priority #5:* Lining up workshops for the future and keeping one's already scheduled on target
- *Priority #6:* Running my businesses. i.e. keeping track of taxes, expenses, etc.
- *Priority #7:* Marketing and sales. Keeping up on social media, blogs, etc.

There's more I do, but if you add it up, it's a lot. So I suggest everyone needs to make a list of priorities and that not only makes you prolific, but on target to achieve what you really want, because #1 priority is your strategic goal.

The key to success as a writer is focusing on that strategic goal every single day as you accomplish your supporting goals.

Special Forces Selection & Assessment thought: Take your eyes off the price and put them on the prize. (well, not literally.)

EXERCISE: List your primary goal, your book goal, your business goal, and a short range goal.

For a long time I flailed about as a writer picking what to write. Just look at my career path. It was only recently, as I wrote myself out of my last contract and was not contracted for the first time in my career, that I stopped and took a serious look at *what to write*. At first I thought, well, I'll use my platform as an ex-Green Beret and write military thrillers. But I had to be honest with myself and realize I didn't feel it. After all, if I was that passionate about the military, wouldn't I still be on active duty?

Then I thought, *well, I'm the only male author on RWA's Honor Roll. I can be the male romantic suspense author.* But again, I didn't have the passion for it. Also, that's kind of counter-intuitive. Maybe there's a reason the Honor Roll isn't full of male authors? This is a case of having to be realistic and honest. After all, men and women look at romance very differently. I remember 200 women hissing at me in Reno at Nationals when Jenny Crusie mentioned my character never said, "I love you" to the heroine in our first collaboration. What we finally figured out is that it's two very different phrases when a man says it and when a woman says it.

So. My platform wasn't working for me in those directions.

I met my agent for lunch and we talked about it. She told me the scenes she had really liked in my last manuscript that were set at West Point. She talked about my platform: military, Green Beret, West Point, and best-selling writer. She said it was very unique. I mentioned the male, romantic suspense thing and her enthusiasm was a bit lacking. Probably because mine was lacking.

I went home and pondered. Then I was emailing a friend whose father had also gone to West Point. And the words Civil War came up. I remember as a plebe at West Point one of the pieces of *plebe poop* (yes, enough said) we had to memorize was: There were 60 major battles in the Civil War. In 55 of them, West Pointers commanded on both sides. In the other five, West Pointers commanded one side. I used to think to myself—maybe that's why the war lasted so long. When the Ken Burns series on the Civil War came out, I used to watch it over and over again. I've walked pretty much every major battlefield of the war. I wrote the Gettysburg Staff Walk used to train officers at Fort Bragg in Special Forces.

I started to get excited.

That's the key to it all.

I loved the HBO mini-series *Rome*. The way the two fictional characters, Vorenus and Pullo, caused pretty much every major event in Roman history from Caesar crossing the Rubicon to Augustus being crowned emperor. I thought it was brilliant writing and an intriguing way to look at history.

So I took that concept—two fictional characters causing major events behind the scenes—added in my fascination with the Civil War; threw in my platform as a West Pointer and a military expert and decided I would write military historical fiction. One of the key angles to it is that every time I watch specials on the war, it's always historians they are using for their quotes. But a military person looks at a battle and war with a much different perspective than a historian.

I started emailing my agent about the idea and doing research. My agent caught my enthusiasm. When she emailed back and said it sounded to her like I was writing something like *Lonesome Dove*, I knew I had nailed it, because that's my favorite book. And the more I researched, focusing on Ulysses S. Grant, the more fascinated I became. I kept finding out more and more things I hadn't known and I started bringing to life two fictional families for my two main characters.

Here's another thing we're going to talk about later: you have to figure out what you're strong at as a writer and weak at. I'm a great plotter. I write great action. I'm weak with characters. By choosing to write historical fiction, my plot is kind of determined. So all that energy

I used to put into plot, is now going into character. When I did the out-line for this book, I outlined the characters first. So sometimes what you need to consider is compensating for what you're weak at as a writer by writing a story that allows you to concentrate on it.

The bottom line though is enthusiasm. I firmly believe that an agent who reps a book she isn't enthusiastic about, but thinks she can sell, is killing that book. An agent has to be enthusiastic. It starts with the author. Then the agent. Then the editor has to share that enthusiasm and so on.

This is the entertainment business. Emotion/logic. Emotion is more important than logic.

When Goals And Plans Must Change

Day to day living throws curves at us. I try to turn those curves around. I live on the 4th largest island in the US—most people don't know that about Whidbey. But, it's 60 miles long north to south, but at some places only a half-mile wide. And we have one, two lane road running the length. So if I want to go to the north end where most stores are, that's the road I have to take. And inevitably I get caught behind some old man in a beat up pickup truck going 35 in a 55 zone, which almost doubles the trip time. I look at it this way: if I were going 55 perhaps I'd be in an accident that's not going to occur now? The same way I look at my dog. He doesn't look like much of a guard dog, especially when he's snoring, but we haven't been robbed. Dogs rarely get credit for what doesn't happen, but if they poop on the rug, we notice them.

I've had goals that didn't work, which I've had to re-evaluate, especially now in the digital age when things are changing faster than ever. One thing to understand is that things are changing exponen-tially, not linearly. Most of the pundits have been wrong about the speed of eBook growth and they are still mostly wrong.

All this goal setting is fine, but I always say, "something you least expect will happen." So always be prepared for unexpected opportu-nities. I didn't know who Jenny Crusie was when I got off the plane going to teach at the Maui Writers Retreat. Jenny was on the same plane and we taught next door to each other. Began talking and two years later had a best-selling book.

So flexibility is important. Just make sure it's an opportunity, not a distraction.

Goals determine the direction of all your time and effort.

Tool Two: Why

Understanding the **WHY** is very important to being a successful author. It's your intent, which is a term I appropriated from a screen writing course I took. As a writer, it is important you understand your personal intent (why) with your overall career goals and plan. Without that understanding, it will be difficult for you to achieve your main goal.

Understanding **WHY** you want to achieve your specific goals will increase innovation and options. Understanding **WHY** allows you to focus on the real goal.

"He who has a why to live can bear with almost any how." Nietzsche

I mentioned blood lessons earlier. Throughout my book *Who Dares Wins*, I always open each Tool (Force in Who Dares Wins) with a historical example of where the **TOOL** was applied or failed to be applied and what the results were. The key to **WHY** is that by knowing why you are doing something, you might end up with a different **WHAT**.

As a writer, you have to use your imagination to solve problems and create intriguing and entertaining books. As publishing changes rapidly, you must know why you want to achieve your goals in order to determine the best path to take to that goal. Those who forge paths first or take innovative routes will have more success than those who follow or try what everyone else is doing.

The following is an example of a soldier who faced a problem and solved it in an unconventional manner, the hallmark of Special Forces.

The first American Special Operations Force was Rogers' Rangers. Robert Rogers was a colonial farmer from New Hampshire, recruited by the British in 1755 to serve in the French and Indian War. Over the course of the following years he formed a unit of colonials called Rogers' Rangers, the first Ranger unit.

Unlike the Redcoat British, they wore green uniforms and utilized unconventional tactics, many of which were written down as Rogers' Ranging Rules, some of which are still used in the current US Army Ranger Handbook.

The Problem

The most significant engagement the Rangers fought was with the Abenaki Indians in Canada. This tribe had been raiding the colonies and was credited during the war with over five hundred kills, mostly of civilians.

Rogers' assigned **WHAT** was, *Stop the Abenaki.*

Notice this was phrased in the negative and it was a reaction. Rogers saw the problem with such a **WHAT**.

Conventional wisdom at the time dictated being on the defensive along the frontier. Rogers realized that would leave the initiative in the hands of his enemies.

The Solution

Rogers had to ask himself **WHY** they needed to stop the Abenaki: to stop the raids and the killings. Conventional wisdom was he could only achieve his **WHAT** by defending the frontier. But Rogers realized the frontier was simply too large to be adequately defended with the scant forces he had. Looking at his **WHY** changed his **WHAT**.

He decided that the only way to stop the scourge was to go to the source. To change from applying conventional tactics to unconventional ones. Others told him that was impossible—requiring forces to venture too far inside enemy territory and leaving the frontier unde-fended (taking too great a risk—being too daring).

Rogers figured that the other side was thinking that way, too, and this would actually increase his Rangers odds of success.

He changed the reactive, *fearful*, **WHAT** verb into a positive action.

I will lead my Rangers to attack and destroy the Abenaki.

His reasoning? If no one considered the raid a real possibility, the enemy wouldn't be prepared to defend against it. He believed it was a risk worth taking.

A successful individual finds new ways to tackle problems, and is willing to take risks to succeed. He is willing to change the status quo.

The Lesson

Leading a Ranger force of two hundred men, he marched into Canada and destroyed the Abenaki village, a feat shown in the 1940 movie *Northwest Passage* starring Spencer Tracy. This was a case of thinking outside of the normal parameters on Rogers' part.

Know Your Why (Intent)

For every **WHAT** (goal) you have, you need to know and under-stand its corresponding **WHY** (your intent). A goal is usually factual and external, while your Why's are emotional, internal things.

When you want to change something, there is always a reason **WHY** you want to change. For many writers, the **WHY** remains buried in their subconscious and does them little good. It's critical to not only bring your **WHY** to your conscious mind, but to write it down to make it real. You also have a **WHY** for every book you write. Consider the **WHY** your motivation.

The intent *(WHY)* and goal *(WHAT)* should be mutually support-ive. Like the goal, the intent should be a positive statement, because we want positive emotions.

When You State Your Goal's Intent, Follow This Format

I am doing X *(goal)* for reason Y *(intent).*

When I first entered the army, the key portion of the operations order was the mission statement, which detailed **WHAT** the unit and members were to accomplish. About five years later, someone came up with the idea of adding the Commander's **Intent** to the mission statement. This considerably improved the effectiveness of an operations order. Since you are the commander of your life (**TOOL EIGHT—COMMAND**), you must know your intent.

Like the goal, the intent should be stated positively. Remember, you will respond better to positive emotions than negative.

Most writers I know want to make money writing so that they can keep writing. So sometimes you can come up with goals by reversing **WHAT** and **WHY**. If your goal is to make a living as a self-published writer, how much money do you need to make a month? Let's say it's $5,000. You have one book. You price it at $2.99. This means you must sell 2,500 eBooks a month to hit your income goal.

Thus your goal becomes: I will sell 2,500 eBooks a month. Why? So I can make a living writing. Why? So I can continue writing.

Intent helps you innovate and motivate. Because intent gives direction but not specific instructions, it allows a large degree of latitude as you further develop your goals and decide how you are going to achieve them.

But how do you innovate?

Try the following processes:

Ask yourself—What if?

Project out courses of actions, much like a chess master, trying to see how they will play out. Enlist the aid of others in doing this. Particularly focus on suggestions that you have a strong initial negative reaction to. Our greatest weaknesses have our greatest emotional defenses built around them and that extends to **WHAT** and **WHY.**

Study and Research

You are not the first one to face whatever challenges are ahead of you. Study how others did it. We'll discuss this more in the next **TOOL** when we cover the Special Forces Area Study.

Take It One Step Further

Yes, maybe you can achieve your goal by doing **A**. But what about if you go beyond **A**? What if what appears to be isn't what is really there? For example, I'm selling quite well on US and UK Kindle. But, taking it one step further, I'm starting to have my books translated into German of DE Amazon and also into Spanish as that's a world wide market. I'm trying to stay ahead of what's happening and constantly look to the future for the next way to succeed.

Reverse Your Thinking

Stop beating your head against the wall. Back off, and walk around the wall and look at it from the other side. Change your perspective and stop having tunnel vision.

What If You're Wrong?

What if your blind spot is controlling you (something we'll cover in **TOOL FOUR: CHARACTER**)? Sometimes, if things don't feel right, you need to stop and pay attention to those feelings. As a writer, I'm not a big fan of the concept of writer's block—I usually call it laziness. However, if for several days in a row I feel disquiet inside about what I'm writing, I take that as a warning that I'm going in the wrong direction. At times like that I put the brakes on and step back from what I'm working on. Drop my preconceived notions.

Keep It Simple

This seems to contradict some of the earlier techniques such as take it one-step further. However, when you are doing something completely new to you, it's often best to keep things as simple as possible so that you can focus on the goal and not get bogged down in the process. For the first book I sold, the only advice my agent gave me on rewriting before he marketed it was to simplify it. He said I had too much going on. He mentioned *Hunt For Red October*. He said that was a rather simple story if you really look at it. I simplified the book and we sold it.

Clear ***intent*** helps you stay consistently motivated. When you use your initiative, your morale inevitably goes up. For example, if your **WHY** for writing is to make a living, knowing you have to pay the mortgage via your writing can be rather motivating.

Sometimes you can use negative emotions as motivations. Many successful people have become successful to prove something to their families. But I think it can be stated in a positive way.

I will become a USA Today best-selling author of cat mysteries, because I want to prove to my family that I am a smart, talented and driven person. Is a positive way of saying I want to do that so I prove to them I'm not a loser, incompetent, pathetic slug.

But you know what? They aren't going to change their opinion of you. But *you* will change *your* opinion of yourself and that's all that matters. And when you do that, then, surprisingly, their opinion will slowly begin to change. A tenet of *Write It Forward* is that we teach people how to treat us.

Here Are Some Examples Of *What* And *Why*

- *Supporting Goal: I will write 1,000 words a day, every day*
- *Why? Because in 12 weeks, I will have a complete first draft*

If you look at that, you could change your goal based on your Why to: I will write 2,000 words every other day. You might need to do this based on your job, your school schedule, etc.

- *Supporting Goal: Finish Write It Forward Critique Group Guide by X June 20XX*
- *Why? Because every time I blog about critique groups it brings a strong reaction, so this is a topic I want to get published and out there ASAP*

Design Boundaries Using Your Intent

While *intent* should be stated positively, you have to be clear about your limits as you define each goal and what you want to *change*.

Successful people should not need much external motivation, but they do need boundaries clearly drawn. You can take any change to an unhealthy extreme.

The key to setting limits is to avoid unexpected, and undesired, results. For example, in Ranger School, the instructors were insistent that the students take action immediately in any situation.

The **WHY** (intent) behind this? In an ambush situation you don't have to time to think—you have to act, and often in a way that is contrary to common sense. The proper reaction to being ambushed is to assault into the ambushing force.

One day a group of Ranger School students were being bussed to a training site. When the bus stopped an instructor jumped on board screaming at the students to get off the bus NOW! The students took action. They kicked out the windows and poured out of the bus. Needless to say they achieved the **WHAT** the instructors were looking for, but not exactly in a way that was appreciated by the chain of command.

Be careful of setting the bar so high, particularly with supporting goals, that you can't achieve them, become discouraged, and quit. One character trait that writers use to beat themselves up with is setting unrealistic supporting goals and constantly failing to meet them. It is very common for us to widely over-estimate how quickly we can finish a manuscript. Be realistic and disciplined.

After deciding **WHAT** someone wants to write a book about, I then ask them **WHY** they want to write about it. What effect do they wish to achieve? What do they want readers to come away with? The same story told two slightly different ways will have a very different impact.

The **WHY** makes the **WHAT** exciting, because it allows for a variety of approaches. Every **WHAT** has been done—every idea has already been told. But every **WHY** hasn't. Being able to give the **WHY** for a book means the author understands the intent he or she wants to transmit to readers. They know what emotion they want the reader to walk away with.

They also have a better understanding of their own motivation for writing the book. Sometimes, they realize that their **WHAT** is wrong because it won't achieve their **WHY**. Then they end up adjusting the **WHAT** so that it is in line with their intent.

EXERCISE: *Taking the exercise where you listed your goals. Next to each goal, list your why.*

Tool Three: Where

Understanding your environment helps you work with it and work with those around you.

You need to understand the personal environment in which you write and the publishing environment in which you want to get published.

Where—The Problem

You are working in conflict with your personal environment. Do you have support at home? Have you carved out an office or a place to work when you do write? When you add any kind of tension to your work environment you are reducing your ability to create. It's important to access your writing space and make sure you create a **WHERE** that is conducive to being a productive writer.

You are working in conflict with the publishing world. One of the things I've learned through my years in traditional publishing and starting my own publishing company is that not every publishing path is the right path for every writer. What you want and what different aspects of publishing can offer you might be in conflict. It's important to understand all of publishing in order to make an informed decision on **WHERE** you want to be in publishing.

You aren't staying current with the changes in reading, writing and publishing. I've always said that content is king and the best thing any writer can do for their career is write a better book. And write more books. That takes time and it also means sometimes we have to turn off the internet. However, we have to make sure we are keeping a finger on the pulse of publishing. We can't make informed decisions about our **WHERE** if we don't know what the **WHERE** is currently doing.

Where Special Operations Tactic—Isolation

When we went on operations in Special Forces we were locked up 24/7 in a secure compound for focus and security. Perhaps you could ask your spouse to lock you in your office for several days at a time so you can focus? They can slip food and water through the door occasionally to keep you alive?

Perhaps not.

But I did rent an apartment in Charleston for four months that had no TV, internet, or phone. And I wrote. I also did it in an apartment on Hilton Head in the off-season when it was quite cheap to rent with the same lack of outside interference and simply wrote for months at a time.

Perhaps the most important thing that makes Special Forces elite is our mission planning before the actual mission. I am a believer in front-loading the work. It's acting. I believe it saves time and energy in the long run. Sometimes you can't fix something that's always moving.

Where Area Study—Avoid the obvious—A Blood Lesson

During the Battle of Antietam, General Burnside commanded the Union left flank on the south side of the battlefield. He received the order *(WHAT)* to cross the stone bridge and assault the Confederate position on the heights above it. This bridge is twelve feet wide. Burnside funneled thousands and thousands of men into that narrow gap. For the Confederates, this presented them with a perfect kill zone.

Burnside never stopped to consider the **WHY** or **WHERE** of his actions. The **WHY** was to gain the high ground on the far side, not control the bridge. And he had tunnel vision with **WHERE**. Because if you go to the battlefield, and stand by that stone bridge, something will occur to you. Antietam Creek can be waded.

This single day continues to be the bloodiest day in American military history. Not even the casualties on D-Day exceeded what happened at Antietam. And a large number of them were because a general didn't consider the **WHY** behind the **WHAT** he was ordered to do.

Area Study

Conduct an Area Study to understand your environment. Do this at four levels: ***personal***, ***book, author career*** and ***publishing***. Do it firsthand. Then do it second hand by studying others who have done whatever it is that you wish to achieve.

Find area experts. You're reading this book because something in my career is matching something you wish to achieve. By reading, going to conferences and networking you are in essence working on an area study.

Personal

You know your Goal. **WHAT** you need to achieve. You know your Intent. **WHY** you need to achieve that specific goal. Now you need to understand the environment in which you will be doing this and your effect on it and its effect on you.

In Special Forces the first thing we did in mission planning after being given our **WHAT** (goal) and our **WHY** (commander's intent) was to conduct a detailed area study. An Area Study is a thorough examination of an operating environment. We wanted to see what elements in the environment would affect us, and, as importantly, what effect we would have on it.

Ultimately, an area study is the same thing as research.

In Isolation (locked up in a secure compound 24/7 to do mission planning) we'd bring in area experts (CIA agents, State Department personnel, people who'd traveled there, locals, academics, etc.) to tell us about the environment we were heading into. It pays to listen to people who are currently at or have been where you want your path to take you.

Talk to other writers at conferences and online who have achieved what you are trying to achieve. Ask them what they do with their personal environment and then study your **personal** environment.

What are your enabling factors? Do you have support? Have you carved out a place to write? Do you carve out time to write? Do those around you respect your boundaries?

What are your disabling factors? Do you have the dreaded day job? Are there distractions that are out of your control? How much time can you devote?

Susan Wiggs, before she was published, when she was a mom and working a full-time day job, locked down nine-midnight every night, seven days a week as her writing time. Her family respected her time and space.

Do you have a place that is designated as your workspace? So when you are there, your family knows you're working? Do you have minimal distractions in your office? I've never had a TV in my workspace. I never answer the phone so that's not a problem (my agent has to email me to tell me she's calling and to answer the damn phone). Elizabeth George has no internet in her office. She has a laptop in the nook off her kitchen where she does her emailing, then she walks out of her house, under an alcove and up the stairs to her office over the garage. When she's in that office, she is working.

My business partner Jen Talty has everything but the kitchen sink in her office. For her, having TV, internet, other things that most of us consider a distraction actually keep her focused because for twenty-years she has been racing between hockey rinks, carrying her laptop with her so she can work just about anywhere, but she needs what she calls *white noise.* Now that her kids are nearly grown, and the house is empty, and she's not racing constantly between hockey rinks the *white noise* or background noise that she plays in her office keeps her focused. The key is she understands how she is most effective and tailors her work environment to increase productivity.

One key to this, of course, is that you are actually working in that time and space. That involves a degree of trust that is needed.

You also need to network and ask for help. I would have never been able to create Who Dares Wins Publishing on my own. It came out of networking and asking for help so that I could achieve my goals.

Book

I know you think you are writing the book that's never been written before, but you're not. Every idea has been done. You're just going to do the idea a bit differently when translating it into story. So find a book like what you want to write and analyze it. Remember, everything in a story is done for a purpose. Also, read first and breakout novels. Reading some bestselling author's latest isn't going to help you much. They could sell their laundry list.

Do a scene break down, focusing not so much on what happens in each scene, but on the purpose of the scene.

Do an overall story break down, focusing on the five elements of narrative structure (initiating event, escalating conflict, crisis, climax, and resolution).

Then ask yourself: How are you going to be different?

One thing I like doing is a plot dissection using DVDs of films and shows. Going to scene selection on the DVD. Note how the scenes are titled.

When I watch something I always note what the opening shot is. Normally, this sets the TONE for the story that follows. Remember the opening shot of Saving Private Ryan? No, it wasn't the old man in the cemetery or the landing craft. It was the American flag. That set the tone for the rest of the movie.

Note the opening scene. This is the most important scene. Note how the protagonist is introduced. Note how the antagonist is introduced. Search for the elements of plot.

As a writer, you are going to read books and watch shows and movies differently than others. You're going to view it from the perspective of a writer and question why it was written in the manner that it was done. You're going to imagine yourself writing it, and questioning whether you would do it the same way.

Author Career

Now that you have done a book dissection, do the same thing with your career by dissecting an author (not literally). Do you want to be the next Amanda Hocking? John Locke? Or do you want to be like Steven King? Nora Roberts? These people are successful for a variety of reasons. Take a close look at what worked in their career. What didn't work. Study their career path and their publishing path. What was their break out book? Who published? Who was the agent? What are they currently doing? What aren't they doing? What from their career path should you emulate? What should you avoid? How are you going to be different?

In life, think of yourself and others in the same way. What is the first appearance you make to others at a conference? As a writer? What tone are you trying to set?

How are others reacting to you? Personally? Professionally?

A Caveat

Publishing has undergone more changes in the last two years than it has in the last fifty years, so studying the traditional career path of someone like Nora Roberts might not work in today's current market. That isn't to say we shouldn't study someone like Nora, but understand there are more options for authors than ever before. Study the paths, and then make your own.

Also, some people who were the first to do something succeeded because they were the first to do something. The second or fiftieth person to do it might not be as fortunate. John Locke sold a million eBooks and got a lot of press. However, he priced them at .99. I'm not sure that will be a successful financial formula for most people. I earned the equivalent of a million .99 cent eBooks when I sold 166,000 eBooks at higher prices with higher royalty rates.

Publishing

Study completely the publishing business & overall entertainment business. Read books on writing by authors, editors, and agents. Follow blogs by anyone who has something you want, says something that strikes a cord, or says something that makes you angry. However, always remember that authors tend to skew what they write in favor of their position. Take into consideration their point-of-view as well as your own.

One way to keep track of publishing is via Twitter if you follow the right people. You can follow agents, editors, authors, etc. Often they post links to articles and blogs that you can click on and read. Follow people who have what you want. Communicate with those who are talking about different publishing paths and learn what is working for them and what isn't. This can be time consuming, but it is also your career and well worth the investment. The key is to limit your time on twitter and other sites. Writing should be your first priority.

Also, networking is a good way to keep on top of the business. I get emails from people all the time letting me know what's going on and I will often pass information to those in my author circle.

The future belongs to those writers who see the changes and potential that technology and society are offering and take advantage of them.

Get HALO Input

HALO isn't the video game: It stands for High Altitude Low Opening parachuting. We jump at 25,000 to 90,000 feet and fall. A long way. Then open the parachute at a low altitude.

This is the term I use when I consult in a business I know little about, like IT. When I walk in to an IT company I know pretty much nothing about how they do things. But that actually gives me an advantage because I have no pre-conceived notions about how things should be done. I am not going to reinvent the wheel, the way most organizations periodically do. I am thinking *outside the box* because I was never in the box to begin with. This is what I mean when I say get HALO input. Find someone who can give you a different point-of-view of your working environment on all three levels.

I've talked to people outside of publishing to get feedback on it. Often the feedback is shock and dismay at the business model. I've discussed promotion with experts who have no idea how the publishing business works. I've taken feedback from those in various positions in publishing. This book is a combination of what I've learned in a few decades of publishing combined with three decades of Special Forces experience.

It helps to understand the history of authors, publishers, agents, etc. How did they all evolve? How are they currently changing? How is on-line retailing changing the marketplace? This allows you to project forward an idea where publishing might be headed and how this might affect the ways in which you set up supporting goals in order to achieve strategic goals.

Study the history of other entertainment businesses. What happened to music when Napster exploded on the scene? How did musicians change their revenue streams to adapt? And how did those who didn't change, fail?

I was talking to a science fiction author who also does a lot of corporate consulting. But he calls himself a *futurist* not a science fiction writer when he consults (goes over better with the brass). He says things are changing exponentially, not in a linear manner. That's something to think about. It's one reason why this book is published in eBook format and POD—it can be updated regularly to keep up with how quickly things are changing.

EXERCISE: *Taking the exercise where you listed your goals. Next to each goal, list your where.*

Resistance Is Futile—The Future Of Publishing

The future of publishing is now. Your career is now. While writing your next book and studying your craft, you must figure out where you fit into the world of publishing. Here are some things that I have studied that directly affects my business model and who I am as an author.

It's important that you consider all your options. The most power we have is the power to say NO.

One thing to remember is that people, to protect their own position, might well be juking the stats, which is a term I took from the great series *The Wire*, and means that people adjust the stats to fit the image they want to present and often the reality they want to believe.

Here Are Some Facts
- *The Big 6 Publishers control 95% of print publishing*
- *Starting in 1995, the print business began contracting*
- *7 out of 10 books printed by the Big 6 lose money*
- *10% of their titles generate 90% of their revenue*

Those facts indicate a reality. The focus for the Big Six is going to be more and more on the Brand Name authors and less on midlist. The problem is where is the next generation of Brand Name Authors going to come from? Amanda Hocking did very well as a self-published author, then St. Martins Press picked her up. Only time will tell if they can break her out and make her a NY Times best-selling author. But you can count on one thing: you will hear more self-publishing success stories because traditional publishing has crunched out their own mid-list author.

The decline of the book chains is the biggest problem for tradi-tional publishers. This also is a game changer for writers and if you want to succeed you have to understand how this change will affect your personal business plan.

Where Goes Starbucks, There Goes The Plan For Bookstores

Did you ever think you'd pay 5 bucks for a cup of coffee?

At the New Jersey Romance Conference in 2010, I heard an editor use the comparison of instant coffee versus brewed coffee when discussing eBooks and print books. She pointed out that when instant coffee first appeared everyone thought brewed coffee was dead. Brewed coffee is still around. Her point: print won't die because eBooks are here. I agree. But I take it a step further. Not only is brewed coffee still here, Starbucks appeared. They made buying a cup of coffee an *experience*. Really, is a cup of coffee at Starbucks that much better than McDonald's? But you can't get that extra-mocha, whatever, whatever, whatever (I get decaf, black, I'm boring) at McDonalds. And it's like, way cool, to be able to stand there and say all those words, like I really know what it means and really like this stuff. I'm too intimidated. We used to chew the instant coffee from our LRRP meals when I was in Special Forces while we were deployed to stay awake. I think I might order some grounds next time I'm at a Starbucks. Of course, I never go there and there's isn't one here on the island so . . .

I digress. So Starbucks blossomed across the country, like zombies with aprons. You can't cross a street without hitting one. But then the economy, like, collapsed. Bummer. And people have had to cut back. And, well, $5 for a cup of coffee, started to seem like, of all things, an extravagance. So Starbucks has been hurting (join the club).

Let's talk bookstores. First there was Amazon. Mail order book retailer. There were grumbles when it first appeared on the horizon back in the days when men were men and the sheep ran scared. It took a slice of the market. Barnes and Noble also opened an on-line store for the Nook. Overall, though, the brick and mortar stores and the on-line stores co-existed, much like, well, the Borg and the human race.

But then came eBooks. A murmur in the distance as long ago as, well, January of 2010. Now it's a roar. Borders isn't solvent. B&N is for sale. Indie bookstores, first besieged by the chains, then the on-line retailers, are now attacked on all fronts and those hardy few who have survived so far, must feel like: Can't a human get a break?

Back to Starbucks. Some smart people over there, right? So what do they have planned to combat their eroding sales? They've come up with a two-pronged approach, which has a single concept at its core: *go local*. Which might also be consider, go niche.

It seems counter-intuitive for a national chain to go local. But what is becoming apparent in retail is that niche is the future. For Starbucks, they're going to serve alcohol. But not Bud or wine in the carton. They're serving local brews and local wines. And the décor of each store, rather than being cookie-cutter same, is going to feature local artists and furniture. They're going to cater to, well, the local people. They're reinventing the *experience*.

I submit where goes Starbucks, there might be a path for book-stores to survive. Serve plenty of alcohol. Well, no. Well, actually, why not? Become a gathering place for like-minded people. But the real thing is: Niche is the future. Not only will indies have to adapt to their area, but for chains like B&N to survive, they must specialize and localize. One size does not fit all. All books do not fit all.

The Espresso machine is a lifeline. Books will be printed in the stores. So anyone can walk in with a thumb drive and print out their Great American Novel and give it to mom and pop and sell three copies to friends who really like them and put up with them. But it's a money-maker for the store. Rack local authors. People who would come in and hang out in the store every so often and talk to readers and interact. Rack books about the area. So if someone wants to know about kayaking in Puget Sound, because they happen to be in a bookstore in a town on the edge of Puget Sound, they can find a book about it. We have to break away from the single buyer in NY determining what goes in every bookstore around the country. We have to get back to local buyers, who have the pulse of the area, who know the readers, determining what goes on the shelves. Make apps where you can sell eBooks by local authors and about the local area. Mirror your physical store on-line.

I'm writing about the future of publishing with eBooks and book-stores, because the key to the future is understanding that the retail outlets for books has fundamentally changed. When the outlet changes, the business has to changes. And that means us, publishers and authors.

I have no doubt that in six months things will change again and we will be reevaluating the future of bookstores, physical books and the role of digital publishing.

Here's the conundrum that NY doesn't want to face: The book business is the same, but the retail business has changed. While NY basically operates the same, the way books are sold has changed dramatically. How many music retailers are left in your town?

The focus is too much on celebrity books in NY and many are money-losers. Much more so than all those midlist authors. The bestseller lists are very deceptive. For example, Kate Gosselin's recent book sold only 11,000 copies yet hit #6 on the NY Times list. Someone is playing with the numbers to make it look good, but many of those big deals are money-bleeders for trade publishers.

The overhead for the Big 6 operating out of the Big Apple is way too high. Heck, even Who Dares Wins Publishing, which we started two years ago and operates out of my bunker in WA (lined with aluminum foil so the Borg can't read my thoughts) and Jen Talty's office in NY, has overhead. We could never operate brick and mortar out of a NY office. So that's something that's going to have to be addressed. I see further major contractions occurring in NY and more outsourcing of jobs to people digitally. The acquiring editors will still be in NY with the agents, but a lot of the other parts are going to be out-sourced.

There Are Two Major Trends In Publishing Going On Right Now

Mid list Authors Going It On Their Own

Actually, this is creeping upward. David Morrell (*not* a midlist author, can we say *First Blood*?) just announced he is bringing nine books from his backlist into print AND his newest title on his own, skipping traditional publishing altogether. This is the biggest name fiction writer to do this. So far. Although J.K. Rowling appears to go offing on her own also. The perception right now is that overall, the quality of self-published books is poor. The reality is, most new authors who have self-published are indeed putting up poor quality. However, there are a number of traditionally published authors who are bringing backlists into print and these are books that have hit bestseller lists. Readers will separate the quality out. Thank you.

Digital Publishing Is Exploding

I've seen it just this past two years. In January 2010, there were many yawns at the Digital Book World conference. Those yawns have changed to expressions of shock. I've been predicting that the change from print to digital would be many times faster than most were predicting and I've been proved right (slight pat on the back). I predict by the end of 2011 we will be close to 50-60% of all books being digital. Especially with all the new e-readers that will be under Xmas trees each year (BTW, the Borg don't do Xmas).

The problem is this: the makers of digital platforms like Kindle and iPad want content. The Big 6 are loath to give digital content to them because they believe it cuts into their hardcover and other print sales and would hurt their own business. So there is a huge divide between the platform makers, primarily Amazon and Apple, and the content providers.

This is the VOID that will destroy some of the Big 6 if they don't exploit it. And also the VOID which savvy writers can fill. Publishers are beginning to do this, but with the Agency model for pricing, it's keeping them from being as competitive as they could be.

Adapt or die.

I Don't Know; I'm Guessing; I Know—The Future Of Publishing For Authors

I gave the keynote at the Whidbey Island Writers Conference in 2011. Like most authors, I have several basic keynotes that I can choose from and then adjust. But I realized after attending the conference for a day, having dinner with the faculty, and listening to everyone, that things have changed so dramatically, that I had to do something different.

So I started making notes with the basic premise that no one really knows what's happening in publishing. Anyone who says they do is deluded. So I wrote: *I DON'T KNOW.* On the left side of the page. Then I wrote: *I'M GUESSING* next. Then: *I KNOW.*

Here, briefly, are the results.

I Don't Know

What the future of publishing is. But 95% of the pundits have been wrong and they will continue to be wrong. Most will protect their turf rather than try to be accurate. Even while they switch deck chairs on the Titanic.

Why there is such a rift between Indies and Trads (my terms, copyrighted). Both are writers. They're just choosing different modes of getting the book out there based on their own circumstances.

What the exact percentage of eBooks vs. print books will be by the end of the year; and by the end of the year we still won't know because people with vested interests will continue to *juke the stats*.

I'm Guessing

In real terms, by the end of the year, 50% of sales will be eBooks. The rep from Amazon sitting at the front table shrugged when I said that. There are a lot of variables. But for fiction writers, in real terms, I believe this will be their number. Non-fiction, texts, etc. will skew the overall numbers. We've found at Who Dares Wins Publishing that we sell 95% eBooks for fiction and 50% print for non-fiction. But we also price eBooks realistically unlike Trads. $2.99 for most of our fiction, with lead books in series at .99.

The role of agents will change dramatically. This was perhaps the first thing I picked up from the agents at the conference. Remember the days of agents swaggering down the hallway, in charge of all they purveyed? It's over. They're scared and confused. Most have little clue what their role will be. A few, Jeff Kleinman was one, have a good plan for the future in re-examining what role his agency would play. Bottom line, as I noted earlier, and will discuss later, is that the midlist is going to die. And agents who subsisted on a bunch of midlist authors are in deep doo-doo.

Agents becoming publishers. It's happening. Two key issues: what can they offer the author that the author can't subcontract out for a flat fee? And what about conflict of interest? The best answer was that agents could now publish those manuscripts they loved but couldn't sell to NY for whatever reason. I think that's valid. If they can hold the line there.

I Know

Niche is the future. Find a specific area and become known as the writer who does that type of book. The Internet has made things more specific rather than broad. *Duty, Honor, Country a Novel of West Point & the Civil War* came out on Tuesday, the 12th of April, the 150th anniversary of the start of the Civil War. The title immediately tells you my niche. Although I think a vast number of people have more than a passing interest in the Civil War.

The Trad midlist will die. The need for an 80% sell through means less copies ordered. Combined with less brick and mortar consignment outlets and the writing isn't just on the wall, it's flashing in neon. Yes, eBook sales will pick up, but check your Kindle top 100 lists. Lots of Indies there.

I control the writing. Above all, writers have to focus on writing the best possible book. Self-publishing is not a short-cut to success. Regardless of mode, readers will walk away from sludge. And 99% of it is that. Just as 99% of what's in an agent's in-box is. I'm not being mean, but realistic.

The same traits that mean success in Trad publishing are the same traits that will spell success in Indie publishing: great writing; persistence; consistency, persistence; business acumen; persistence; great writing; willingness to adapt and change quickly to the changing publishing world.

Bottom Line

Things have changed so dramatically it's palpable at every industry event I attend. Things are changing exponentially, not linearly, so a writer needs to really focus on where things could possibly be in a year, not where they are now.

And in a year, I can guarantee they will be very, very different.

Lead, Follow Or Get The Hell Out Of The Way

My motto at *Write It Forward* is appropriated from the Infantry: Lead, follow or get the hell out of the way. Authors produce the books. Readers consume the books. Everyone else is in the middle. And therefore, very, very nervous. Because, in essence, the only two parts of publishing that are absolutely necessary are writers and readers. Yes, books need to be edited, marketing needs to be done, etc. etc. But much of that work can be contracted out.

It used to be publishers controlled distribution. That was their lock. If an aspiring author asked me if a publisher was legitimate or not, I told them to go to their local bookstores and ask the manager if that publisher had distribution to the store. But today, everyone has access to distribution with eBooks.

I use to tell aspiring authors to never self-publish fiction. The reality is 99.5% of self-published fiction will fail. But when I began Who Dares Wins Publishing, I had to re-evaluate. The reality is 99.5% of queries to agents fail. So the odds of succeeding at self-publishing at little cost via eBooks and print-on-demand, are pretty much the same. There *are* going to be success stories coming out of the ranks of new authors among the self-published. So why not double your chances of success by continuing querying while at the same time self-publishing and self-promoting? Some will say that agents won't look at material that's been self-published. That's called an ignorant agent. The game has changed and either change with it or get the hell out of the way. BTW, the self-promoting is something traditional publishers and agents are saying authors have to do anyway. In fact, it gets to the point reading all these blogs and tweets from agents/editors, that I ask. If I, as the author, have to do all this stuff, what the heck are you doing?

The self-published who do succeed. But there is an inherent flaw in that. A self-published book that sells 5 or 6 thousand books will get interest from the Big 6 and literary agents. Except when that author crunches the numbers, the publisher will have to guarantee *4 times as many readers* in order to break even with what that author is making on their own. It's a Catch-22.

All in all, I think it's an exciting time to be an author with lots of opportunities. But only if you educate yourself and stay on top of the latest developments and trends. This is one of the major goals of Write It Forward. Authors, you must assimilate faster than publishers, bookstores, and agents are, if you want to survive. Embrace the technology and use it to your advantage.

Area Two: Who

Who You're Going To Win With?

Most Importantly: **YOU**.

You must understand **CHARACTER** and how it affects you as a writer. You must understand **CHANGE** and how **COURAGE** can facilitate true change.

We start with **CHARACTER** so you understand yourself and others. Then learn what true **CHANGE** is and how to accomplish it. And, finally, learn how you can utilize **COURAGE** to conquer fear and be the writer you want to be.

Character is the essence of a person. Your character is made up of both your strengths and your weaknesses. It's important to understand yourself, especially your blind spot, before taking action to achieve your goals. Your blind spot is wrapped around your deepest fears. A successful individual doesn't ignore fear, but rather faces it, plans for it, and factors it into their life with courage. If you want to Succeed the *Write It Forward Way*, facing and planning for fear is essential.

"Not choice, but habit rules the unreflecting herd."

–William Wordsworth

The tools in *Write It Forward* help you consciously change your habits, and through the Circle of Success, your writing and your life. You have to train yourself to question your repeated behaviors.

I'm not talking radical, burning bush type change that will occur instantaneously. This book teaches you incremental, day-by-day change—what the Japanese call **kaizen** (continual improvement). Small changes, added together, day-after-day, that lead to new habits and a new life. Your focus will not only be on the end result, but on the continuous process. When you finish Tool Nine, you won't be done, but you will be on the path to change.

I focus a great deal on fear for someone who is teaching about success, because changing habits and becoming successful is not for the faint of heart. Most of us like comfort and the illusion of security. A little change brings discomfort. A lot of change brings fear. There is a very thin line between discomfort and fear. The more willing you are to face and conquer your fears, the further out you push that line and the more change you'll bring about as you venture into your Courage Zone, which increases your Comfort Zone. In fact, as you'll learn, there are benefits to fear.

Tool Four: Character

"Invincibility depends on one's self; the enemy's vulnerability on him."

Sun Tzu

What Is Character?

CHARACTER is the combination of qualities or features that distinguishes one person from another. Character is the key to *Write It Forward*. Looking at the world around you differently than others, and understanding yourself as an author. Having the self-confidence that comes with an integrated character that you clearly understand, both good and bad, is key.

Too many people are locked into a limited worldview because their own character keeps them from seeing the true nature of the world around them. Your view of others and the world around you is tainted by your point of view. If you understand your point of view, you'll have a more realistic view of yourself and others. Writers have to do this two ways: for the characters in their books; and for the people they are going to work with in the publishing world.

Exercise: Define yourself in one sentence.

Which of the following areas did you use in your definition?

Work? Position? Family? Background? Schooling? Education level? Marital status? Sexual orientation? Age? Race?

Do you define others by the same, or different, terms? You are now getting an idea of your point of view. Remember, everyone doesn't share your point of view. Understand that your point of view shapes the way you view others and makes your reality different than their reality. The best reality to be in is the one based on action.

Special Forces Assessment And Selection Thought

The only person holding you back is you; everyone else is merely watching.

Study your *own* actions to understand *your* **CHARACTER**.

In Special Forces, we learned that a person tends to show his true nature by his actions/reactions during a crisis. You learn a lot about people by observing what choices they make under pressure.

Actions speak louder than words. Actions are a **WHAT**. As we learned in **AREA ONE**, you should also try to figure out the corresponding **WHY** for each **WHAT**. It's important to understand the same **WHAT**, done for two different **WHYs** (intent) will make the actions very different.

Not only must you observe an action and the intent, you must have an understanding of the environment the action is taken in *(WHERE)* to help you interpret motivation *(WHY)*.

In schools such as Special Forces Assessment & Selection, Ranger School, Scuba School, Airborne School, etc. this basic tenet of acting under constant stress and crisis is drilled into students while they are performing under extreme pressure. Incoming plebes' first summer at West Point is called *Beast Barracks*, which gives you an idea of the environment they face.

The harshness of this kind of training is often explained by saying the instructors must first *break a person down*, before they can rebuild them. I believe this method actually strips away any façade a person has and drills down to his True Nature.

Understand Your Character Or True Nature

Those whose true nature cannot handle a specific situation will either quit or not make the cut. People who do not succeed in Beast Barracks, Ranger School, Special Forces and SAS Selection & Assessment, etc. are not bad people or failures. They just do not belong in the environments those training programs are designed to prepare them for. In the same way, you have to understand your true nature, so you can choose the path of change you are capable of completing. Keep in mind that this harsh phase of breaking someone down is a form of making the person surrender. The more the person fights the change, the harsher the resulting process. To change, you have to surrender to the fact that who you are now and what you're doing isn't working. And that the more you fight yourself, the more that fight will be projected into your world with harsh, negative effects.

I was watching *Kitchen Nightmares* the other night and the owner of the restaurant had invited Chef Ramsey in. Ramsey evaluated and made some suggestions. It was amazing to watch how hard the owner resisted every single suggestion; and how he was the one who was screwing everything up. The chef was begging the owner to the point of tears to take the advice. The owner's girlfriend was also in tears. Slowly, but surely, the owner accepted he was wrong and changed. But it took a lot of tears and a lot of cursing.

Your Primary Motivator

Victor Frankl, in his book, *Man's Search For Meaning*, focuses his entire process of logotherapy on the concept that strong people have a readily identifiable primary motivator that allows them to overcome great obstacles and succeed. He believes that people who have a meaning in their life can transcend suffering and find meaning. They can live well in the face of fear.

Frankl was a concentration camp survivor and in that hell on Earth he forged his philosophy. He believed that the last human freedom, when all else was taken away, was ". . . to choose one's attitude in a given set of circumstances."

Some people might already have their meaning of life. Many others need to find one. Frankl found in the concentration camp that a lot of people simply tuned out of life and vegetated, eventually dying. Those who survived were the ones who made a victory of challenges.

In Special Forces training, the candidates are forced to perform under extreme duress. They not only accept challenges, but conquer them. They're forced to dig deep, to find what really motivates them. The desire just to wear a Green Beret and call themselves Special Forces doesn't work. Those candidates who want the superficial aspects because of the way others will view them fall to the wayside. In the same way as an author, I've noticed many people want what they think the lifestyle of an author is, but they don't have the wherewithal to be an author.

Knowing your primary motivator is as key to being an author as the theme and intent of the books you write will reflect that motivator.

Levels Of Motivation

Just like characters in a novel, you have levels of motivation. When you look back at your goals, you need to sift through them to find your true motivations, your true **WHY**, because, this may cause you to reword or re-orient your goals.

What Do You Want?

This is the conscious WANT that is in the forefront of your brain. As a writer, it might be, *I want to be a NY Times best-selling author.* It's what you are consciously aware of.

But what do you really want?

Hmm. Let me think. *Why do I want to be a NY Times best-selling author?* Is it the prestige, which means external recognition? Or is it more than that? Do you connect that with making money? Is it the money?

But What Do You Need?

If you want that goal in order to make money, is it the money itself? Or what the money brings? Many writers I know need to write. In order to write they must make money. Thus, what they state as what they want, actually masks what they need. Like an iceberg, our wants are visible, but our needs are very deep and much more substantial.

So what do you NEED?

Successful Character Traits

Special Forces Assessment and Selection is based on successful character traits. Studying the character traits of successful writers will help you understand your True Nature.

Open Mindedness

How willing are you to change? Are you willing to learn from any source that helps you improve yourself? If you are not where you want to be, then you must change, rather than waiting for the world to come to you.

Because guess what?

It isn't.

So how do you use being open-minded to change?

You need a . . .

Willingness To Surrender When Wrong

To change, you have to be willing to say the three hardest words for many people, *I am wrong.* Followed by, *maybe I'm not doing this the best possible way. Maybe I can learn to do this better.* You must be willing to surrender. You must be willing to change based on the feedback you receive from the exercises in this book.

A Stanford psychologist, Carol Dweck, found something interesting when studying talented people and how they performed. She discovered those people who believe they were born with all the talent and intelligence they will ever need approach the world with a *fixed* mind-set. They rarely change. Why should they?

Those who believe that they weren't born with everything they need and can expand their abilities and become better, approach the world with a **growth** mind-set. Guess which of the two are more successful? The latter reach their creative potential, while the former rarely live up to their potential. In Special Forces, volunteering for the training and successfully completing it indicates a willingness to grow. I found the same to be true of writers: I often saw extremely talented writers fail, while those with lesser talent but greater open-mindedness and perseverance succeeded.

There are so few successful writers, because few writers are willing to learn and change. Change is also difficult because it requires not just change in your action but also in your way of thinking.

Part of what can motivate you to try change and also stick with it are two apparently paradoxical emotions . . .

Desire & Contentment

Desire is the stick that drives the successful to achieve more. The carrot. What do you desire? What do you want? What do you need?

Contentment is the reward for achieving your desires. You can't constantly be in a state of desire. Every once in a while you must get to that point of achievement, or frustration will rule. For a person to enjoy life, there must be a degree of contentment in the here and now. What is the point of being successful if you can't enjoy it? Every once in a while you need to focus on what has been achieved.

Too much of either is dangerous. They feed off of each other. For many years I've joked that I never take a day off, but, unfortunately, it's true. And it's burned me out. It's hard to change habits, as we all know, but it is one area I'm working on.

So let's talk about motivation a bit. First, the carrot and stick method doesn't really work anymore. The old maxim was: reward an activity and you'll get more of it. Punish an activity and you'll get less of it.

That's wrong. Studies have proved that often linking a reward to an activity dampens enthusiasm for it. It can go from being a creative, fun experience, to becoming work. This often happens to the midlist writer who is under contract. Instead of creating, they're working. An experiment with artists by the Harvard Business School found that those artists working on commission produced less *artistic* work than those artists not working on commission. The pure joy of creating was lost to a degree when there was an external outcome attached to it. This has powerful implications when you think in terms of multiple book contracts for authors.

Not only is creativity hurt, but the desire to do good can be diminished with rewards. Paying people to donate blood has proven to lower the number of people donating blood. People prefer to volunteer to do that. Thus internal motivation is more important than external.

On the good news front, researchers have found that goals we set for ourselves are beneficial, but goals set for us by others, are not. This is why I try not to listen to agent and editor panels at conferences. Their lists of 'do' and 'don't do' are irritating. An author's job is not to make their life easier. An author's job is to create.

Researchers have also found two types of people: **Type X** and **Type I**. **Type X** are motivated by external things. **Type I** are motivated by internal things. A writer must focus on being **Type I**. Because in publishing, you don't control many of the external factors. Whether a traditional publisher picks you up or not is not in your control other than by the quality of what you write. What I'm finding interesting is that by founding my own publishing company, it reduces my stress level as I write. Because I know that even if my agent can't sell a book, I can still publish it. True, I won't have a many thousands of copy print runs, but I can put it out there. Also, I've had thousands of copy print runs and watched books die a slow, agonizing death of neglect.

If you get a $10,000 advance for a mass-market paperback, you need to sell (at $6.99, 8% royalty) 17,882 copies to earn out. But what if the print run is only 25,000 copies in today's tough economic times? And average sell through is 50%? Let's say you do very well, sell through at 70%. You've sold 17,500 copies. And not earned out. In publishing eyes, you've failed.

But every day I can check my Kindle account, my Smashwords account, my Lightning Account, my iBooks account, and money is coming in. I used to say that even though I'm making less, it's more satisfying to see progress. However, things have changed once again the steady stream of money coming in is more than what I might have gotten on a single book deal AND I still get the satisfaction of seeing the progress. In fact, I'm making more now as an indie author than I ever did as a traditionally published author. Also, on those days or weeks where we see a drop, we can **ACT** by re-evaluating our business plan and continue to push forward instead of **REACTING** the way I was doing when dealing with traditional publishing and writing from one contract to the next. This is a change in going from traditional to non-traditional publishing that works in the author's advantage.

A successful person needs to balance desire and contentment.

As part of desire and contentment, you must also be able to *close doors*. We waste time pursuing too many options. One of the purposes of the first Tool of this book was to help you lock down your **WHAT**, your goals. The opposite of that is discarding goals that aren't what you really want so you can focus on those you do. Buridan's Ass is named after the French philosopher Jean Buridan but is based on a theory by Aristotle of a man who is incapable of action because he is as thirsty as he is hungry and he is placed exactly in between drink and food. In Buridan's Ass, a donkey enters a barnyard. The donkey is hungry and thirsty. There's hay to the left and water to the right. The donkey remains frozen, unable to choose one, afraid that by doing so, it will not get the other. Eventually the donkey starves to death.

Ever felt like that donkey?

Closing doors can give you great focus. When Cortez arrived in the New World he had eleven ships and less than a thousand men. His **WHAT** was to seize the treasures of the Aztecs. His **WHY** was positive for him, but not so great for the Aztecs. He pursued his **WHAT** with single-minded ruthlessness: he issued a famous command: "Burn the ships". You can imagine this wasn't very popular with his men, but it was a great source of motivation: they had no choice now. They had to succeed. He had removed an option; closed a door.

As Erich Fromm noted in his classic book Escape From Freedom, when we have too many options, we don't focus on the ones we should.

Patience And Self-Discipline

Too many people rely on the outside world to enforce patience and supply discipline. A successful person internalizes both traits. The Special Forces Qualification Course takes roughly a year. Interestingly, the average time many authors spend on a novel is a year. Neither of these are a recipe for instant gratification. Taking a year to achieve a major goal is something that requires a great deal of patience and discipline.

When I taught martial arts, the majority of the new students quit after the first month. Students came in and wanted to become Bruce Lee rolled into Jackie Chan, all within a couple of weeks. When they realized it would take years of boring, repetitive, very hard work, the majority gave up. It doesn't take any special skill up front to become a black belt—just a lot of time and effort to develop special skills. The same is true of pretty much anything you want to achieve.

If you are patient enough to do the long-term work, you will pull ahead of the pack and become successful. Which means you must have a long-term perspective of your major goals.

This goes back to what we discussed in the first **AREA** and the importance of focusing on your strategic goal to help you get through the mundane day-to-day work.

To remain focused on a long-term strategic writing goal, you must accept that the pay-off usually comes later, rather than sooner. Delayed gratification is one of the keys to self-discipline. Self-discipline is one of the keys to developing self-confidence.

One way to make a long-term goal achievable and not overwhelming is to break it down into smaller milestones or goals that are closer and more easily achievable. For example, in the Q-Course there are numerous phases. As a Candidate passes each phase they feel a sense of accomplishment, leading to passing the entire course. Also, if a Candidate has a problem in a particular phase, there is always the option to have them redo just that phase, rather than the entire course. As a writer, I can break a book down to a number of pages to write per day or however many chapters per month.

An Active Imagination

In many ways writing is like a chess game: to be successful, you have to think a half-dozen moves ahead, while considering the impact of your opponent's decisions (and in life, your environment). This means choosing a successful strategic direction, given a very large number of variables. And as you've just learned, your plans must take into account your personality.

Make your creative plans based on acting within your character—much like chess strategy is dependent on a piece being capable of a specific type of move—and then, once you've mastered that, press the limits of your character to expand your capabilities—venturing into your Courage Zone. You'll get an idea of your character template shortly and how to expand on what I call your Comfort Zone so that you are capable of more and more *moves*.

Set your imagination free to plot numerous paths. From these, based on all the variables facing you, you can choose the one that stands out above the others—the successful or critical path.

As in chess, a successful person in life must be able to see a problem in its entirety, and then be able to break a solution down into manageable steps (moves). You must be able to see beyond the current move, to each move's implications.

Don't get tunnel vision. For example, a professor from the Colorado School of Mines, teaching at West Point once presented his students with a problem to test their imaginations.

A two-foot metal pipe is welded vertically to a steel plate. It is just barely wide enough to slide a ping-pong ball into. The class's job was to get the ball out of the pipe without damaging the ball. The only tools given to the students were a pair of pliers, a coat hanger, a magnet, and a comb.

The professor let the class war-game this problem for a while, and then listened to various proposals; none of which worked. His solution used none of the tools listed—he'd given them as distracters. To get the ball out, simply urinate into the pipe until the ball floated out. But because we'd been given those items, every solution focused on using those items rather than the problem.

Do the same with your plot. All the things you put into a book should serve multiple purposes, not just one. Do the same with your business plan.

The Ability To Set Goals

In **AREA ONE: *Wins***, you learned the importance of specifying your goals, understanding ***WHY*** you want to achieve them, and studying the situation in which you want to become successful.

One thing you can do without is procrastination. It comes from two Latin words:

Pro: For.

Cras: Tomorrow.

Not only must you set your goals *(WHAT),* you must also set deadlines for your goals. People who form and write down firm deadlines get better results than those without.

Passion

As an author and publisher I work in the entertainment business, which is an oxymoron. Entertainment runs on emotion, while business runs on logic. But no matter what business you're in, emotion plays a significant factor that can't be quantified.

Why is a certain book a bestseller and another not? Why does one movie break box office records and another doesn't? If the answers to these questions could be put into a formula, then everyone would be following the formula. Then every book would be a bestseller and every movie a blockbuster.

Why do we do things that ultimately hurt ourselves? In lucid moments we know they make no sense. But then we go out and do whatever it is anyway. In these situations, emotion is overwhelming your logic.

Many individuals and organizations don't value the power of emotion.

It is important to realize there are two sets of norms in your life: Social Norms and Market Norms. Understand clearly the line between the two and don't blur them. Your personal relationships belong in the realm of social norms. Your business relationships are usually in the realm of market norms.

When a social norm collides with a market norm, the social norm is the loser. Conversely, social norms are more powerful than market norms. This comes into play in **WHO DARES WINS**, because, interestingly enough, Special Forces and writing operate more on Social Norms than Market Norms. Jobs where one is asked to put his or her life on the line can't function well under Markets Norms—how much can you pay someone for their life? Thus police, firefighters and military tend to operate under Social Norms where pride in profession, teamwork, care for comrades, and a sense of duty are more important than money. Publishing also works more on social norms, because people are willing to spend a year writing a book with no guarantee of publication or success. Why do you think we have bestseller lists? Why do we have author photos and bios? It's not just marketing. It's similar to the way the military has medals.

In your life, recognize that the way you interact with other people emotionally—social norms—is much more important than any market norms interaction.

Anger And Guilt

Two emotional blind spots for many people are anger and guilt. These emotions are often indicators of a weakness you need to deal with. And until you do, that weakness can keep you from exploring your full potential, and can derail you from achieving your goals.

Whenever you experience anger or guilt, focus on what is going on. Figure out when the emotion is appropriate, and understand when it isn't.

Anger and guilt are often brought about by things that shouldn't trigger these emotions. Frequently, these emotions are responses that became a habit in childhood. While both are necessary at times, many people are so consumed by these negative emotions that they become shackles around their lives.

When a person gets angry about something someone else is doing, it is often a sign of a flaw in the angry person's character. When a person feels guilty about something happening in another person's reality or even their own, it is often an inappropriate response to reality. We use these two in Special Forces training as an indicator to build a person's character.

Flash Points

During prisoner of war (SERE-survival, evasion, resistance and escape) training run by Special Forces at Camp Mackall, outside of Fort Bragg, one thing the instructors do to participants is try to find their flash points—what makes a prisoner react angrily or with guilt.

If captors can find a prisoner's flash point and exploit it, they can delve deeper and find the prisoner's greatest fears. This allows the captors to break the prisoner much more quickly. Left unchallenged, your mind can become its own kind of prison, where your flash points and greatest fears will work against you with increasing frequency.

The key to the training is that once the candidate goes through this experience and is aware of his or her flash point, they can strengthen themselves in those areas and are less likely to react in the future and in a real SERE situation.

Anger and guilt spring out of fear, usually on a subconscious level. You'll learn later that working through your mind's defense barriers is the second step of emotional change.

Character Templates

Successful writers adopt a psychological structure for character types—so they can better understand their own character and others'. Fortunately, structures already exist and have been thoroughly developed by behavior and motivation experts. I recommend studying various templates and recommend the following:

Archetypes

Archetypes are useful in seeing gender differences. In the columns below look at the same person, differentiated by a genre label.

GENDER DIFFERENCES

Female	Male
Boss	Chief
Seductress	Bad Boy
Spunky Kid	Best Friend
Free Spirit	Charmer
Waif	Lost Soul
Librarian	Professor
Crusader	Swashbuckler
Nurturer	Warrior

There are also archetypes in creativity. Men tend to be linear thinkers. Women are more circular thinkers. When Jenny Crusie and I co-write, she explains it by saying we're heading across an open field and I'm focused on the far side saying, "we must get there." And she's hanging on my leg saying, "hey, look flowers! Trees!"

Another thing that struck the two of us in our creative processes was that she did a collage for each book while I did a story grid. We finally figured out why each of us needed these different tools. Jenny is an excellent detail person. But she has a hard time 'seeing' the big picture of the book. So she has a collage she can look at it to focus her back on the big picture when needed. I'm very good with big picture, but lousy with details. So I need this excel spreadsheet to the left of my keyboard that I fill out as I write. It keeps me oriented to the details.

Are you a pantser or a planner? Do you outline? Or do you just write? I submit that you will outline your book the way you organizes your daily life.

Below is a comment from a psychologist who specializes in creative people. He focused on women because he was speaking at the Romance Writers of America National Conference, where the majority of participants are female.

"Because writing is such a solitary, inwardly directed job, a woman writer really has to carve out a space for herself to work. Which means she has to take it seriously. As John Gardner once said: 'If you believe what you're doing isn't important, you're right'." Dennis Palumbo.

This brings me to an interesting lesson I had to learn. *We teach people how to treat us.* In my interactions with others, the one constant is me. The variables are the other people. So if people tend to treat me the same way, I have to focus on me. I'm teaching them how to interact with me.

For example, I noticed that when I went into a restaurant or a bar, I tended not to get served. I'd go to the outdoor bar at Harbor Town with Rex, my big doofus of a dog, and the waitresses would run over and ooh and aah over Rex, bring him a bowl of water, then walk away, without taking my order.

For a long time I externalized this. I thought there must be something wrong with others. Then I figured there must be something wrong with me because I was the constant. But I still externalized it in a way, because I put it down to, *there's just an aura I project.* That's true. But I still didn't focus on the reality of my actions. Once I focused on what I was doing to bring this reaction from others, the problem, and solution, was simple. I was failing to make eye contact, something learned from riding the New York City subway to high school. You *do not* make eye contact on the subway.

Once I identified the problem and implemented the solution, I began to be treated differently.

This is important for writers, because when we begin to promote ourselves, we must remember that we are interacting with others and we are going to get responses based on the way we treat people. Part of building a platform is to take into consideration the image you are projecting to others.

Profiling

Character type profiling is regularly used by Special Forces and law enforcement; a fact that has been repeatedly fictionalized in pop culture books, movies and television. A profiler examines the results of an action and works backwards, trying to come up with the character type that would perform such an act.

When Special Forces was founded, a list of character traits for the type of person needed to operate in this elite unit was drawn up based on experiences in guerilla warfare and covert operations in World War II. Then they went and looked for those types of people.

John Douglas (*Mindhunter*) was one of the founders of the FBI's Investigative Support Unit, which specializes in profiling. A key to profiling is that it shows that people have character traits that dictate their actions. This is understandable because most of what we do is habit. Also, the brain doesn't start from scratch in every situation—we have imprinted stereotypes that shape our actions. We consciously control very little of our day-to-day life and decision-making.

John Douglas and the other founders of the Behavioral Science branch of the FBI began their study of profiling by going to prisons and interviewing every living serial killer, to see what type of person was capable of doing such horrible acts. Patterns were identified in the killers' backgrounds, their thought processes, the way they conducted their crimes, etc. In the same manner, you can study patterns in your and others' daily lives.

You can determine which of your life patterns are positive, and which are negative, then work on getting rid of the negative ones, and replace them with positive ones.

By profiling yourself, you can make more conscious choices, rather than react emotionally and out of blind habit.

Additionally, a common complaint among writers is: Where do I find the time to write? Profiling can help solve this.

An exercise you can do on your own

For the next 24 hours, write down everything you do. Simply list every action without comment and how much time you spend on each. Let the list sit for several days. Then look at the list with an open mind. Describe what kind of writer would do these things?

Then answer these questions
- *Is this the kind of writer I want to be?*
- *Are these the things I really want to be spending my time doing?*
- *Are my actions going to support my strategic and supporting goals?*
- *Am I using my time most efficiently?*
- *When is there time to write in all of this?"*

"We first make our habits, and then our habits make us." John Dryden.

The Myers-Briggs

Many of you have probably taken a Myers-Briggs assessment. It was developed in the dark days of World War II when it was necessary to assess a large number of people quickly in order to position them in the best jobs for their personality.

It is not a test, but an indicator of Character type. There are four areas to it, with two possible orientations, which totals sixteen Character types. To give you a brief idea where you stand do the following four exercises. While this does not replace the standard test (which can be found on-line or in a book *Please Understand Me: Character And Temperament Type*) the following exercise can put you in the ballpark for our purposes:

Character exercise:

Pick A or B for each of the four areas that best describe you:

AREA 1

BLOCK A	BLOCK B
Act first, think later?	Think first, then act?
Fell deprived if cut off from world?	Need private time to get energized?
Motivated by outside world?	Internally motivated?
Get energized by groups?	Groups drain your energy?

AREA 2

BLOCK A	BLOCK B
Mentally live in the now?	Mentally live in the future?
Use common sense for practical solutions?	Use imagination for innovative solutions?
Memory focuses on details and facts?	Memory focuses on patters and context?
Don't like guessing?	Like guessing?

AREA 3

BLOCK A	BOCK B
Search for facts to make a decision?	Go with feelings on making a decision?
Notice work to be accomplished?	Focus on people's needs?
Tend to provide an objective analysis?	Seek consensus and popular opinion?
Believe conflicts is all right?	Dislike conflict and avoid it at all costs?

AREA 4

BLOCK A	BLOCK B
Plan detail before taking action?	Comfortable taking action without a plan?
Complete tasks in order?	Like to multi-task?
Stay ahead of deadlines?	Work best close to deadline?
Set goals, deadlines, and routines?	Like to be flexible and avoid commitments?

THE RESULTS	
1A=Extrovert (E)	1B=Introvert (I)
2A=Sensing (S)	2B=Intuition (N)
3A=Thinking (T)	3B=Feeling (F)
4A=Judging (J)	4B=Perceiving (P)

List out your letters. You are one of the filling sixteen Myers-Briggs Character Types.

MYERS-BRIGGS	
INTP=Architect	ESJF=Seller
ENTP=Inventor	ISFJ=Conservator
INTJ=Scientist	ESFP=Entertainer
ENTJ-Field Marshall	ISFP=Artist
INFP=Quester	ESTJ=Administrator
ENFP=Journalist	ISTJ=Trustee
INFJ=Author	ESTP=Promoter
ENFJ=Pedagogue	ISTP=Artisan

The first letter is extroversion vs. introversion. This is how you view the world. E's are social while I's are territorial. E's prefer breath and a wide variety while I's prefer depth and one on one. E's tend to be externally motivated while I's tend to be internally motivated.

The key is where you get energy. Jenny Crusie and I were trudging through some airport on week 4 of our never-ending book tour. And I mentioned how rock stars go on tour for months, but writers can barely handle a couple of weeks. The difference is most rock stars are extroverts and gain power from the crowd while writers get drained by crowds.

Also, rock stars use a lot of drugs and have groupies.

Writers go back to the hotel room, order room service, and turn on their laptops.

I also have a theory that some of the best keynote speakers are introverts, because they pump power into the crowd. But introverted keynoters are rare, as I learned when I presented at the National Speakers Association a year ago.

There are people who are very balanced. Researching Ulysses S. Grant, I was amazed to see his two best subjects at West Point were mathematics and drawing. Whole-brained. He was also a horse-whisperer. 75% of people are E's, while 25% are I's.

The second letter is Intuition vs. Sensation. N's tend to be inno-vative while S's are practical. This area is the greatest source of mis-understanding between people. 25% of people are N's while 75% are S's.

The third letter is Thinking vs. Feeling. T's analyze and decide in a detached manner, while F's analyze and decide in an emotional manner. Basically T's are logical while F's are emotional. It's 50-50 in the population but overall more women are Feeling and more men are Thinking.

The fourth letter is Judging vs. Perceiving. J's like closure while P's like things open-ended. J's like the result while P's like the pro-cess. It's also 50-50 in the population.

Looking at your Character type can give you an idea of yourself. It shows you how you interact with other people. How you take in infor-mation. How you make decisions. How you view processes.

It is very important to look at what the exact opposite of your character type is and you'll get an idea of your blind spots and your weaknesses. In fact, I believe focusing on what you *aren't* is more important than understanding what you are. Because it's what you aren't that you will probably have to change to some degree.

For example, INFJs, (labeled author) usually fear speaking, sales. ESTP (promoters) have a hard time sticking to long-term tasks.

Note the author vs. promoter and architect vs. seller (agent). This is why your agent might be great at selling, but not so great at designing a career plan for you. That's your job.

I began my second career as an author being a plot-driven writer. It took me ten years and a lot of hard work before I saw that I was going about things the wrong way. In the same way that in Special Forces we put people first, a writer has to do the same thing in novels—put the characters first.

People relate more to people, not things.

Think about your favorite novel. What do you remember the most? It's most likely the characters, not the plot. When writing a novel, I want my main character to have 'arc'. This means the character changes. Just like you will change by implementing the tools in this book.

In a novel, if you thrust the main character into the climactic scene as he exists at the beginning of the novel, the character should fail. The journey that character goes through in the story should change him, so that when he faces the antagonist in the climactic scene, the main character will win.

The same change will be required in your life, if you want to succeed in the goals you committed yourself to achieving. You must step out of your comfort zone and do things that are inherently against your nature so you can conquer fear and succeed.

By the way, the exercises you've done in this tool are the same exercises I use to develop characters for a novel.

We will cover the traits/needs/flaws diagram in the next section so you can try to hone in on your blind spots.

I think we all use our writing to project unconscious issues. In the same way most people who become psychologists are doing so in order to figure themselves out.

The MBTI can easily be manipulated—also, we act differently in different situations. I'm an introvert but can also give a keynote before 500 people.

We teach people how to treat us, whether we realize it or not. I've recently applied some Sun Tzu to my life: where the enemy is strongest retreat. Let them have what they think they want, while I outflank them and achieve what I want. Direct confrontation ends up with both sides not achieving what they want.

The tests are indicators and can be manipulated if you know what they are looking for, as they basically ask the same questions over and over again, just in different ways.

I've found that some really innovative people make things work on two levels: the conventional and the unconventional. In Special Forces we fought in *unconventional wars*. But first, during the Qualification Course, all the training was conventional. In fact, what a lot of SF is doing right now, is training foreign troops in conventional warfare via unconventional means.

I think not only listen to what others are saying, but try to figure out WHY they are saying it. What true message are they trying to get across? Sort of a combination of **TOOL 2 *(WHY)*** and **TOOL 7 *(COMMUNICATE)*.**

There are ways to generate creativity. A lot of writing is subconscious and emotion fueled. It's not logical.

Given that, what can block us creatively?

Focusing too much on the strategic goals to the detriment of creativity. The first thing we do in *Write It Forward* is set that strategic goal and then say everything we do has to support that. That's true. But you can focus too much on it, that you don't focus on day-to-day things you need to do in order to achieve it. Also, that goal can overwhelm your creativity. Sometimes we set goals for ourselves that we subconsciously know we can't achieve in order to make failure a self-fulfilling prophecy. I almost always project that I will finish a manuscript faster than I do.

Another character issue is being a perfectionist/expert. I know many writers who spend way too much time on research. They want to be sure they are absolutely correct in all their details. While details drive the story, the heart of it is the characters and the reader's connection with them.

You can also get too caught up in the business side of things. Yes, you have to keep track of things and try to stay ahead of the changes. But you can also spend too much time on the business side, you lose the excitement of the creative side.

We can trap ourselves with a brand. Branding is important and takes a long time to build. Make sure the brand you construct, though, is what you really want to do. Because once you've built it, it is really hard to change.

How else can we increase our creativity?

Breath. Slow down and breathe. We are always under deadline. But sometimes you just have to stop. I am almost always going 100 miles an hour and have to force myself to stop and step back every once in a while.

Do something physical. My writing day is broken up by a workout around noon. I take Cool Gus and Sassy Becca out to the woods for a run. It's a good break from sitting at the desk all morning.

Embrace not knowing. I'm a fan of outlining and planning but there are times I have to accept that what I know isn't enough. That there is something else out there. Once you accept you don't know everything you need to know, those things will start to come to you.

Keep track of your dreams. I keep a recorder next to me when I go to bed. If I wake up with a dream or thought, I record what it was. I've found if I don't do that, I won't remember the next morning.

Remember, in *Write It Forward* you will have a catastrophe plan. Everything is not riding on this particular manuscript. Allow yourself to accept this one might not be the one, but it's the path to the one.

Try something different. Add an edge to your writing. If you never write something humorous try writing a humorous scene.

You need to understand your character in order to understand all the great advice you receive via this book, blogs, workshops, conferences, your friends, your family, etc. I think authors need to evaluate themselves according to the Three P's.

Platform, Product, Promotion—The Three Author Variables

Closely monitoring the publishing business I see many different paths and approaches suggested to aspiring authors. It's a very confusing time and there's a lot of advice out there, much of it contradicting other advice. This *Write It Forward* program focuses on the author. As part of that, I'm going to try to sort this out for you with a template you can use: the three Ps.

There's a simple reason for all the conflicting advice. No two authors are exactly the same. Should you go for traditional publishing? Should you self-publish? Should you go home? In an effort to bring some clarity to the issue, I offer up three variables and examine how they affect the way a writer should view getting published and, more importantly, their writing career.

The variables and definitions are:

Platform

Name recognition is what people think of, but there's more to platform than that. Are you an expert in your field? Do you have a special background that makes you unique? Everyone has some sort of platform, even if it's just your emotions, exemplified by Johnny Cash in *Walk The Line*, mining his anger into art. I use the film clip of his audition at the beginning of my *Write It Forward* workshop, book and presentation, and show how quickly he changed, mined his 'platform', and was on his way to becoming a star. All within three minutes.

So don't get close-minded on platform. However, for traditional publishers, they immediately are looking at name recognition (brand) and ability to reach a market (which ties into promoting). However, with the explosion of eBooks, there are other paths to take.

Product

The book. Yes, Virginia, you need a book. Or a proposal for a non-fiction book. This is your content. Most authors become totally fixated on content, while ignoring platform and promotion. Do so at your peril. On the flip side, the most important and powerful marketing tool is a good book.

Promotion

Do you have the ability to promote? Do you have access to promotional outlets? What is your unique hook or angle that will get you attention? I will discuss promotion more about this under **COMMUNICATION**.

If you consider three variables, with a sliding scale from *none* to *the best*, you end up with an infinite variety of authors. To simplify matters, let's go with *weak* and *strong*. This gets us down to eight possible types of writers.

Strong Platform	Strong Product	Strong Promotion
Strong Platform	Strong Product	Weak Promotion
Strong Platform	Weak Product	Strong Promotion
Strong Platform	Weak Product	Weak Promotion
Weak Platform	Strong Product	Strong Promotion
Weak Platform	Strong Product	Weak Promotion
Weak Platform	Weak Product	Strong Promotion
Weak Platform	Weak Product	Weak Promotion

If you're in the latter line, fughhedaboutit as we used to say in the Bronx.

But for all the other combinations of the three P's, we can all see a type of writer. Where do you fall?

These are not discrete entities. They all rely on each other. You have to consider that promotion is based on platform and product.

Product is often based on the platform. If you have a platform you will most likely write a book mining that platform (if you don't, well duh).

There's a degree of luck involved in promotion. Going viral. But luck goes to the person who climbs the mountain to wave the lightning rod about. It's called hard work. One key lesson we've learned at Who Dares Wins Publishing is consistency and repetition of message is key. Slack off for a week, and fughhedaboutit. In the first six months of 2011, I missed doing my promotion SOP in social media only one day, and that was because I was traveling and didn't have access to the Internet.

Product is the one you can improve the most by working on your craft. However, you can improve both platform and promotion, which many authors ignore. Become known as THE writer of that type of book. That's platform.

Promotion is often hard as the Myers-Brigg INFJ is labeled 'author' while the exact opposite, ESTP, is labeled 'promoter'. We HAVE to get out of our comfort zones as authors. In *Write It Forward* I emphasize doing the *opposite* of your Myers-Brigs personality type.

The advent of social media is a boon to writers. We can actually do promoting from the safety of our offices. *We Are Not Alone: The Writer's Guide to Social Media* lays out an excellent plan for that, but, as the author, Kristen Lamb, clearly writes, figure out your platform and your product (content) first. Too many authors leap blindly into social media and I watch 95% of them wasting their time and energy flailing about inefficiently. Small point she makes: do you have your book cover as your avatar on twitter? A picture of your cat? Fughhedaboutit. Read the book.

The bottom line is, as a writer, you have to evaluate yourself on the three P variables and figure out what type you are. Then approach the business accordingly, while at the same time, working hard to improve in those areas where you are weak.

Tool Five: Change

If you aren't where you want to be, then you must **CHANGE**. How many people do you know who have really changed? Your answer will ultimately depend on what you think change is.

I can tell you what change isn't. **CHANGE** is not simply thinking differently. Thinking doesn't change anything in the world outside of your mind. Here comes my next paradox, though—the first step of change is to think differently. Note, I say it is the *first step*.

An official definition of change is to make or become different. There's a big difference between the verbs make and become. It's the difference between being ordinary and successful.

Make it externally imposed.

Become is internally motivated.

The successful become.

Can people change? If the answer to that is no, then there is no purpose to this and we all might as well quit now. There's good news, though, since history has proven that people CAN change. However, change is very difficult and very few people can manage to achieve great change in their life and sustain it. These people are the successful.

Do you have confidence that you know how to **CHANGE?**

Special Forces Assessment and Selection Thought: To become is hard; to be is even harder.

The Three Steps Of Change
1. You have a moment of enlightenment
2. You make a decision to take a different course of action from what you have been doing
3. Commitment to your decision leads to sustained action, which brings about permanent change

EXERCISE: Which of the three parts of change do you think you have the greatest difficulty with?

Most people tend to say *Sustained Action*. However, if you really examine yourself, you might find that isn't your real problem. For example, I have a hard time making a decision. Once I make a decision, I'm very good at sustained action. *Here is the key:* you must not only figure out what step of change you have the most difficulty with, you also have to determine why that step is your problem. The reason I have problems making decisions is because I'm *afraid* of making a mistake. So do you see how the underlying fear is the thing you must uncover? We'll discuss fear more under the next **TOOL***: COURAGE*.

Moment Of Enlightenment
To have an MOE (moment of enlightenment) you experience something you never experienced before. Or you experience something you've experienced before, but it affects you differently than ever before. This is the classic *light bulb going on*. By itself, it is not change, just a momentary awareness.

Most of what you do day-in and day-out is habit. And habits are extremely difficult to change. To have a moment of enlightenment you have to become open-minded, one of the character traits we've already talked about. You have to be able to change your point of view—your perspective. You must get out of your everyday rut.

Break out of your comfort zone and look at something in the opposite way you've always looked at it. Entertain the possibility that what you think is your greatest strength, might actually be a defense (a blind spot) layered over your greatest flaw that can blind you to opportunities to change. Reverse thinking is a very strong tool to help find moments of enlightenment.

Denial often blocks MOEs.

Angers stops MOEs when it is actually an indicator of an MOE.

Bargaining dilutes MOEs.

Moments Of Enlightenment Comes In Several Ways

- *A new experience you've never encountered before affects you*
- *Something you've experienced before affects you in a new way*
- *You witness someone else doing something differently, and it affects you*

A successful person is always looking at the world around him, trying to see previously unseen possibilities. The more information you gather, the more possible courses of action you have.

Many times, those who surround us are trying to give us the gift of enlightenment, but we ignore their message. In a marriage, often one partner is trying to give the spouse enlightenment, but the message is ignored. At work, a co-worker might be pointing something out to you, which goes by you without notice. In your critique group or with your beta reader, they might be trying to point something out to you, but you ignore it or don't get the real message.

Some Examples

A moment of enlightenment for me came in the Special Forces Qualification course. During a Phase I patrolling exercise, we spent several February days being rained on—not exactly the most comfortable experience. Several students had to be medevaced out for hypothermia. When the exercise concluded, we were given an eight-hour break, still out in the middle of the woods, before moving on to the next training exercise. We no longer had to be supporting.

It was still pouring and cold. Most students huddled, shivering and sopping wet, underneath their ponchos. I watched, though, as one student ignored the elements and walked about, gathering firewood. He piled it up, and then worked hard to get a fire started. After quite a bit of effort, he had a roaring blaze and a grateful circle of students standing around, warming themselves and drying off.

My moment of enlightenment? When miserable, don't just hunker down and ignore the environment—instead, take action to make the environment better. Over the years since, that realization has served me well in numerous situations. Thinking about being warm and dry while wet and cold did nothing. A decision was required, followed by a course of action—in this example, literally going against the elements.

I gave a keynote at a conference and spoke to a senior executive at Amazon afterward. He told me one key he'd found to success was to be persistent. To not take no for an answer. I used to take 'no' as an end, not a beginning. I became persistent at pursuing rights to my Area 51 series, sending an email every week to my editor and a snail mail letter every week to the rights person at Random House. Eventually, one day, I got an exasperated email from the editor asking if it would make me happy if I got the rights to *all* my books back from them?

In essence, they gave me back the rights to what I consider my retirement.

Make A Decision

Because of the Moment of Enlightenment, a decision is made. Remember, it is not necessarily a good decision, but it's a decision nonetheless.

You then are either:

- *Stuck with the decision (externally imposed change) or*
- *Stick with the decision (internally motivated change)*

By itself, a decision is not change, just a fleeting commitment.
Bargaining can dilute a decision.
Depression can cause you to give up on a decision.

Decision-Making

There are two systems for decision-making: intuitive and reasoning. Intuitive deals with emotion. It is fast, automatic, but has a slow-learning curve. Reasoning is emotionally neutral. It is slow, controlled, and rule-governed, but this approach can be rigid.

Is the majority of your decision making based on intuitive or reasoning? Knowing this about yourself is key in understanding how and why you make decisions and why sometimes you make the wrong decision.

EXERSICE: A bat and ball together cost $1.10. The bat costs a dollar more than the ball. How much does the ball cost?

If you used intuitive decision making then you would say the ball costs .10. But it really costs .05.

EXERCISE: Flip a coin six times. Which is more likely?
Heads-heads-heads-tails-tails-tails
Or
Tails-tails-heads-heads-tails-heads?

Neither of the above is more likely to happen. However, if you picked the second, you are using the misconception of chance.

Sports players, like chess players, have to trust intuition for speed of decision-making. Writers have to trust their gut, but then go back and use their rationality to edit the work.

Do A Sustained Course Of Action

Don't expect immediate, burning-bush change as soon as you've made your decision. While this does happen, it is very, very rare. Change is a slow process that requires dedication and commitment and most of all Sustained Action. Success in publishing is a marathon, not a sprint.

Because of the decision, behavior is changed. The changed behavior is sustained long enough to become a new habit. In the military, this is called training.

- *Sustained action leads to change*
- *Sliding back on the five stages stops this*
- *Acceptance is not easy—your reality has changed*

I've had varied teaching experiences: Special Forces team, JFK Special Warfare Center, Masters Degree in Education, Martial Arts teaching, writing teacher, universities, conferences, organizational speaker, etc. I can't count the number of times I heard someone say, "I always wanted to write a book, but . . ." or "I always wanted to get a black belt, but . . ." or "I was going to try out for Special Forces, but . . ."

The successful don't do buts. The successful are not wanna-be's. They learn. They decide. They act. They sustain the action.

The Five Emotional Stages Of Change

Once you've accepted the need for change and surrendered your current position and mental outlook, you've intellectually accepted the change. You then change your actions. As you change it affects you emotionally over time.

Emotional change can take years but you have to stick with it.

Change requires going through Elizabeth Kubler-Ross's five emotional stages.

1. ***DENIAL:*** there is no problem or need to change
2. ***ANGER:*** how dare someone, including me, say I'm not doing it right

3. **BARGAINING:** maybe if I can change some small things it will make a big difference
4. **DEPRESSION:** yes, I do really need to change the big things
5. **ACCEPTANCE:** which does lead to real change

These are also the editorial stages when the manuscript comes back from the publisher. There is no problem with the manuscript. How dare you say there is something wrong with the manuscript? Maybe there are some problems, but certainly not as much as you list in the editorial letter. Damn, I've got a lot of work to do. I do it.

I try to go through all five stages before opening the FedEx package (note how they never FedEx checks).

Train For Change

The military is very big on training because it wants to change people from civilians into soldiers. The goal of Special Forces training is to change regular soldiers into elite warriors. You can use some of the Special Forces training templates to achieve sustained change in your writing, in your career and any facet of your life.

The history of Special Forces Assessment and Selection (SFAS) goes back to the formation of Delta Force, and before that back to the British SAS (Special Air Service, from which I get the motto: Who Dares Wins). SFAS was created in an attempt to learn from history and others who'd already done what Special Forces needed to do, to avoid reinventing the wheel.

According to official doctrine, SFAS tests an applicant's supporting skills, leadership, physical fitness, motivation and ability to cope with stress. This is done through over-land movements, psychological tests, physical fitness tests, swim tests, runs, obstacle courses, small unit tactics exercises, land navigation exercises and individual and team problem solving.

Aspiring Special Forces soldiers coming to the course are advised that their mind is their best weapon. That being physically fit isn't going to get them through. Applicants should be prepared for anything.

In this type of training, expectations are unclear. There are unknown variables and standards. This places students under stress—as you've already learned, an excellent evaluation technique to see if someone can be successful. I've seen students become so frustrated that they quit. This also happens to many writers as they try to negotiate the insane maze of publishing. No one can make you quit, except yourself.

There's none of the harassment or *false* stress that's used in many training situations. Once you've been through a *getting screamed in your face* training environment, the second time you experience it, the effect is almost ludicrous. In the same way, as you spend more and more time in publishing you can weather rejection and misfortune more easily. That's not to say they don't sting, but you soldier on. When you are testing the elite the stress has to be real. Focus on the times in your life when the stress was real and examine your actions.

The publishing business is full of unknowns, so the more you understand the way stress affects your ability to make decisions, the more you will be able to navigate through all the choices and make the necessary changes and adjustments to your overall plan.

Goal-Aligned Training/Business Programs

Just as your goals must be aligned to support one another, your training/business plans must be goal-aligned. Often you have many things you want to achieve. You must prioritize your goals and intents—again, in writing. When designing your training programs and business plan, this priority must be clearly understood, so your time is well spent and your training for one goal doesn't become counter-productive to another.

Goal-alignment must happen every day. As a martial arts student and then instructor, I learned that the key to success, as is the case in many other training fields, is repetition. You have to do the same kick again and again and again—correctly—until one day, after thousands and thousands of kicks, the motion becomes instinctual. I bump my promotional thread on Kindleboards (and I have around 40) every seven days like clockwork, regardless of whether I see any result or not.

In Ranger school, the proper response to an ambush is drilled into students day after day—because it goes against your survival instinct to charge into an attacking force. Repetition is the key to training for the right goal at the right time. Follow your goal-aligned training and business plan every day—do it right every day—and sooner or later you will achieve a new habit to replace the one you want to change.

As a writer, when I start a new book, I post my one sentence original idea on my desk and read it every day to keep myself on task and avoid going off on tangents.

In my publishing business I write down goals and then email them to my business partner almost daily. She does the same. Every week we match up what we've done with what needs to be done differently and adjust accordingly. We are careful to make sure we aren't doing those things that didn't work for us and focus on the things we can change.

There are a lot of reasons why Who Dares Wins Publishing has been so successful and one of those reasons is that both myself and Jen Talty changed not just the way we think, but the way we interact in the world of publishing.

How Do We Know When Someone Has Changed?

We see it. They act differently.

Sometimes the step of change that is our strength is compensating for our weakness and hiding it. I used to think Sustained Action was the hardest step. For many it is. But it isn't mine. I'm very good at sustained action. I used to run marathons—an extreme form of sustained action. My problem is making a decision. I have a hard time making a decision because I'm afraid of making a mistake. So I have to focus on decision-making in both my writing and my business all the time.

The Five Percent Rule

Is perseverance more important than talent? We've already discussed this. Yes.

I have found, and statistics back me up, that five percent of people are capable of *internally motivated* change. People who lose weight—within five years, 95% have put it back on. AA has a recovery rate of 5% after 5 years. 5% of students who came into the dojo stuck around long enough to earn their black belt.

Many people are wanna-be's.

You cannot do three steps on your own. You can't get through five stages on your own. You will need to ask for help. This is where writers groups, family, friends, etc. come in.

You've got to have internal motivation as a writer, because even very successful writers get little external feedback.

A key to change is learning. Be willing to learn from any source at any time. If you don't like something, but it's successful, study it. If it makes you angry, really focus on it.

If you're not where YOU want to be, YOU have to change.

If someone else has something you would like to have as part of you, ask for help.

"Talent is less important in film-making than patience. If you really want your films to say something that you hope is unique, then patience and stamina, thick skin and a kind of stupidity, a mule-like stupidity, is what you really need." Terry Gilliam.

As an author you must develop a very thick skin. And while you must pay attention and learn and be willing to change, there are also times when you just have to put your head down and bull your way through to success.

In my book **WHO DARES WINS**: *The Green Beret Way to Conquer Fear and Succeed,* which a lot of this comes from (some verbatim), I advise people not to read the book all at once. It will overwhelm. Same thing as when you go to a writers' conference. Sometimes you get so much information it overloads your brain. It takes months for it to all settle in.

Also, timing makes a difference. The first time I read Don Maass's *How To Write The Breakout Novel*, it all seemed rather simple. But re-reading it a few years later, when I was in a different place, it looked a lot different.

I teach some things now that are 180 degrees out from what I said a few years ago. That should scare you. For example, I used to be very against *coincidence in plot*. Now, I'm not so against it. I think it has a place and purpose and is called fate. I explain this in *The Novel Writers Toolkit*.

I used to be against self-publishing fiction, but now I view it as a reality of the business.

I've changed.

I truly believe the writers who will succeed in the rapidly changing landscape of publishing are the ones who are the quickest to change which has an intrinsic internal logic.

I once had one student say, "I really need to change and it's going to be hard." That's a negative statement and self-defeating. Then they turn it around to either, "I really need to change and it's going to be do-able and fun" or "I really need to change and it's going to be easy."

Those don't work either, because change is not necessarily fun or easy.

The better way to state change is like this, "I really WANT to change and it's going to be challenging but ultimately rewarding in ways I can't even begin to see now."

This gives you a positive statement, control over the want, and also adds a nice piece of mystery to it which can be kind of fun. Because change does lead you down a forest path where you might think you know the goal, but you truly don't.

Another problem I run into is when someone says, "I define myself through others." I think most people do and it is a flaw because others don't spend that much time defining us. Only YOU can define YOU.

One thing that comes up at every workshop, conference or class that I have ever attended or taught is writers feeling like a fraud.

I think a lot of writers feel that. And it's almost worse when you get published. You sit there and go: geez, they're paying me money to sit at home in my sweats and make things up. Who the hell am I?

I was sitting at an outdoor café in Denver years ago. It was a weekday lunch and I was watching all these people sharply dressed in business outfits walking by. I turned to the person I was with and said, "I feel like a fraud. These people are leading *real* lives, and I'm living in this weird, alternate reality." She turned to me and said, "Most of these men, if they knew what you've done and achieved in your life, they'd wish they were sitting in your chair with those experiences." It was a real moment of enlightenment for me. I have not led a boring life. FYI, I bought my first suit last year—saleswoman said I was the easiest sale she'd ever had. I said I need a suit. I need a tie. Socks. Shoes. Belt. I bought it all. Now I wear that suit to conferences. Well, everything but the tie. The shoes are very comfortable. More on fraud and the imposter syndrome in a bit.

Another thing I have to do every once in a while is to break out my resume and take a look at it and think, *if I saw this from a stranger, what would I think of them?*

And if you want your resume five years from now to look different, to say Published Author, and present the platform you want, then you need to start changing NOW.

Tool Six: Courage

"Life shrinks or expands in proportion to one's courage."

Anais Nin

EXERCISE: In one word, record what you believe to be your greatest character trait.

What Is COURAGE?

COURAGE is the state or quality of mind or spirit that enables one to face danger with self-possession, confidence, and resolution. It is the ability to do something that frightens one. **COURAGE** is strength in the face of pain or grief.

The key to conquering fear is to expand your comfort zone into your courage zone. **COURAGE** is acting in the face of fear. Remember, your strongest emotional defenses are built around your greatest weaknesses. Thus, often what we think is our strongest character strength is covering up our weakest.

What Is *FEAR?*

It is a feeling of alarm or disquiet caused by the expectation of danger, pain, or the like. A key word there is expectation. This is why 90% of people never follow up when an agent requests a partial during a conference one-on-one. We are afraid they will reject us, so rather than face the reality, we never send it in.

Fear is an emotion. It often stems from uncertainty and uncertainty is a fact of life. So many people live their entire lives in fear. It is often the primary motivator for people, as we require base needs to be fulfilled first.

The Problems With Fear

People tend to ignore fear as a factor. There are times that fear is a perfectly normal reaction to a given situation. If we are afraid then we must factor the fear into our thinking. However, there are times where we must discount our fears as being unreasonable or we tell ourselves there is nothing to fear.

People don't understand what they really fear and why they have that fear. I mentioned before that I have a hard time making decisions, but until I understood that the reason I had a hard time was because I was afraid of making the wrong decision I was unable to commit to decisions. Once I understood what I really feared and why, I was able to take a step back and commit to things like writing historical fiction and moving forward with Who Dares Wins Publishing.

People tend to downplay the benefit of fear. Fear isn't necessarily negative and often times there are reasons to be fearful. Once the feeling of fear is upon you, you must evaluate it and make a decision on how to deal with the fear. There is a book called *The Gift of Fear* where the author discusses the times when we should pay particular attention to it.

People don't know how to conquer fear. Most people think of conquering fear as the ability to overcome something such as a fear of heights and it can be that, but more importantly it is conquering those more insidious and less obvious fears that hold us back from being successful in our lives. My fear of making the wrong decision held me back in my career as a writer. Once I made the commitment to my own publishing company, that's when we saw a huge shift in our sales. I acted instead of reacting and I did it in the face of fear.

Fear—The Solutions

Fear must be factored into your life and mission planning. We are all afraid of the unknown. If we factor fear into our lives and into the planning of our careers, our books and all aspects of our lives, we have a better chance of overcoming those fears and achieving great things.

You have to figure out what it is you really fear and why you have that fear. This can be a difficult and sometimes daunting task, but it can also be a very rewarding and freeing experience. Often times the fear is worse in our heads than it is in real life.

The benefits of fear need to be understood and utilized. Fear is not your enemy unless you let it. Fear is an indicator. It means it's time to take a step back and look around and re-assess where you are, where you want to be, and how you are going to get there.

You must learn, develop, and practice techniques to conquer fear. When we factor fear into our lives we are better able to develop the necessary techniques that will allow us to overcome those fears and thrive in our lives.

Many of you have seen Maslow's Hierarchy Of Needs. The key to the hierarchy is that we can't go up the scale if base needs aren't being fulfilled. Being a writer is at the Esteem level (caring about something outside of yourself that gives purpose).

- Self-Actualization
- Esteem
- Belongingness and Love
- Safety Needs
- Physiological Needs

I heard David Morrell (*First Blood*) speak and he advised writers not to quit their day jobs, because then they would write scared. And he believed scared writing isn't good writing. That concerned me until I remembered that writing *was* my day job. And I had no intention of quitting it.

"Fear is the mind-killer. Fear is the little death that brings total oblivion. I must face my fear. Must allow it to pass over me and through me and where it has gone, I must turn the inner eye. Only I will remain." Dune, by Frank Herbert.

We all have Blind Spots in our personalities. These are character flaws that are often rooted in fear. Our needs produce blind spots. It's important to understand a need is not a want. A want is something you can control. A need you cannot control. As an author, make sure you know your wants and needs and your blind spot.

Our strongest defenses are built around the blind spot. Therefore often the blind spot is the part of character thought to be the strongest. Denial defends blind spots and justifies needs.

Blind Spots Are The Making Of Tragedy

The diagram below is just an example, but you can take any character trait and uncover what the corresponding need is. Then push that need to an extreme and you will find the potential flaw.

Blind spots arise out of a number of factors:

Loss Aversion

People are often more motivated to prevent losses than to achieve gains. Casinos count on this. It can also produce tragic results. The deadliest air crash ever was partly the result of loss aversion when the pilot of a Boeing 747, anxious to take off, crashed into another 747. He didn't want to have a late departure. He was also the most experienced pilot in his airline.

Planning Fallacy

Underestimating task completion times. Writers are notorious for this. I'm not where I want to be with my work in progress; the reality is, for 20 years, I've never been where I planned on being with my writing, until recently when I began applying the principles of Write It Forward and began planning realistically. Someone asked me in a workshop: how do we get more prolific? I think it comes down to bum glue. You just have to put the time in at the keyboard. Or pencil and paper. Or recorder. There is no substitute for actually writing. On the flip side, though, don't constantly beat yourself up for being *behind*. Try to set realistic goals.

Wishful Thinking

The formation of beliefs and the making of decisions according to what is pleasing to imagine rather than reality. This is where many publishers are right now in response to eBooks. I just don't believe the $14.99 eBook is going to last. At the same time, indie authors have to face the reality that when publishers do wake up to the price problem, the competition is going to get harder.

A mindset that I have seen destroy many an author's career is the thought they "have it made". That they've reached a point in their career where they can put it on cruise control and things will continue to work as well, if not better, than they have been. Every author I've seen do this ended up destroying their career.

Need For Closure

Can you live with ambiguity? Writing a novel is living with ambiguity for a long time. Until you write the words: The End. Some people can't stand it and need things to end. So they end them too quickly. I used to not do enough rewriting. I would know there were parts of the manuscript that needed work, but I just wanted it done. I wanted it out there on the market. Now. There is no Now in publishing.

Illusion Of Transparency

Overestimating other people's abilities to know us and our ability to know others. When all you have are the printed words, you're very limited in what people can get from you as a writer. This is the reason that, as a writer, you must push your agenda, sometimes to the point of being irritating to others, because you can't assume that others know what you want. They know, perhaps, what *they* want.

Negativity Bias

It takes five compliments to make up for one negative comment in a relationship. As writers, we tend to obsess over negative criticism and ignore positive feedback. Checking Amazon reviews constantly can be very disspiriting. Same with checking sales figures on a daily basis if you're self-published.

Fashionable Darkness Bias
This is an interesting one, especially for writers. Novels, movies and shows that have a dark ending are thought of as being more literary than ones having the HEA—happily ever after.

The Amazing Success Formula Fallacy
This is something many people who want to become writers fall for. That success happens overnight. My friend Susan Wiggs had her last book debut at #1 on the NY Times best-seller list. In 2010. Her first book was published in 1988.

JK Rowling was an amazing success, but there's only one of her. There's only one Dan Brown.

The Real Life Up Ahead Fallacy
That what you're doing right now is the preparation for your *real life* that will come some day.

Going back to previous exercise, write down the corresponding need and potential blind spot to your greatest character trait.

How To Deal With Feeling Like A Fraud

Writers aren't the only creative people who experience these feelings of being a fraud or concerned the world will found out they are an imposter.

"I still think people will find out that I'm really not very talented. I'm not very good. It's all been a big sham." Michelle Pfeiffer

"Sometimes I wake up before going off to a shoot, and I think, I can't do this; I'm a fraud. They're going to fire me. I'm fat. I'm ugly . . ." Kate Winslet.

First, it's important to realize everyone has doubts. What's debilitating is if you feel like you're the only one. You're not. Studies of people who are identified as feeling like frauds range in percentage, but the overall number is high. In fact, studies show that many of the most successful people feel it the most. The higher up the ladder one goes, the greater the fear is of 'being found out'.

Doubts can be good. They can inspire you to become better. If you combine your doubt with your passion, it can motivate you to great success. Studies have shown that women who score high in the area of feeling like a fraud tend to compete harder to compensate for their doubts. Interestingly, men who scored high on feeling like a fraud, tend to avoid areas where they feel vulnerable to avoid looking bad.

There is a thing called **The Imposter Syndrome**. Many people have great difficulty internalizing their accomplishments. All those things they've achieved: degrees, promotions, publication, best-seller lists, etc. are thrown out. Instead, people look to external things like luck and contacts that had little to do with their own efforts as the reason for the successes they've achieved. Inside themselves, many people feel like they are *fooling* everyone. What's particularly hard about that is the more success a person achieves, the greater the fear of being found out as a fraud becomes.

Some ways to gauge how much of The Imposter Syndrome you have: The more you agree with the following statements, the higher your IS:

- *I can give the impression I am more competent than I really am*
- *I often compare myself to those around me and consider them more intelligent than I am*
- *I get discouraged if I'm not the 'best' in an endeavor*
- *I hate being evaluated by others*
- *If someone gives me praise for something I've accomplished, it makes me fear that I won't live up to his or her expectations in the future*

- *I've achieved my current position via luck and/or being in the right place at the right time*
- *When I think back to the past, incidents where I made mistakes or failed come more readily to mind than times when I was successful*
- *When I finish a manuscript, I usually feel like I could have done so much better*
- *When someone complements me, I feel uncomfortable*
- *I'm afraid others will find out my lack of knowledge/expertise*
- *When I start a new manuscript, I'm afraid I won't be able to finish it, even though I've already finished X number of manuscripts*
- *If I've been successful at something, I often doubt I can do it again successfully*
- *If my agent tells me I'm going to get an offer on a book, I don't tell anyone until the contract is actually in hand*

Women tend to agree more with IS statements than men. They also tend to believe that intelligence is a fixed trait that cannot be improved over time. Women who feel like imposters tend to seek favorable comparisons with their peers. Men who feel like imposters tend to avoid comparisons with their peers. Often, they work harder, even in the wrong direction, so other people won't think them incapable or dumb.

Overall, people who feel like imposters are constantly judging their success against the achievements of others rather than viewing what they do as an end in itself. For writers, this can be very dangerous, because there will always be someone who is doing *it better* or *is more successful.*

A technique to fight feeling like a fraud is to use a version of my HALO concept on yourself. Start from way outside yourself, diving in until you can see things clearly. Step outside and view things as if you are a stranger to yourself.

Examine your resume. Look at what you've accomplished in life. Ask yourself what kind of person would have achieved these things? Could a fraud have done this? When I query a conference to teach or apply to lead workshops or do keynotes, I have to send my bio. Sometimes I stop and read it and ask myself: what would I think of this person, if I didn't know them, but just read this?

Focus on positive feedback. However, don't ignore negative feedback. The key is not to let the negative overwhelm you. While I look at Amazon reviews and rankings for business reasons, I don't focus on them anymore emotionally. First, you have to realize that only a certain segment of the population posts reviews on Amazons. It's not a true sample of the population. Also, the motives for posting reviews often have nothing to do with your book.

Another interesting angle to feeling like a fraud is a study found that when people with high Imposter Syndrome scores were asked to predict how they would do on an upcoming test, they tended to predict they would do poorly when around others. However, privately, they predicted they would do as well as those who had low Imposter Syndrome scores. What this means is some people adopt self-deprecation as a social strategy and are actually more confident than they let on. They lower other people's expectations and also appear humble. I believe, though, that doing so, can also subconsciously lower your own expectations and become a self-fulfilling prophecy.

On the flip side of feeling like a fraud, some people tend to over-rate their abilities. A self-serving delusion is almost necessary in this world to just get out of bed in the morning at times. But take it too far and it can destroy you.

The bottom line on dealing with the 'feeling like a fraud' is to internalize more of your accomplishments. Remember the *TO DO/DONE* list? Occasionally stop and take a look at what you've achieved.

In the military, we always joked that everyone had a *Look At Where I've Been And What I've Done* wall in their home, covered with photos, plaques, flags, etc. Those walls serve a purpose, though. (In our A-Team room, we had to wire down all the knives, hatchets, edged weapons that were usually on the plaques because people might start using them after a few beers.)

I have all my published books in my office on the top of book-cases, all lined up. The row is over three feet wide. I look at it some-times to fight the feeling that I can't write another book, that I can't get published again.

You have to believe in yourself. If you're unpublished, walk into the bookstores and don't let all those published authors overwhelm you. Use them to motivate you. Tell yourself you belong there. I always look and say, "hey, these people got published, why can't I? I've never even heard of 90% of these people."

List your accomplishments. They can range from a picture of your fam-ily, degrees achieved, awards won, whatever. Put them where you write. Use them to remind yourself that you are not a fraud. *YOU ARE REAL.*

Overcoming adversity is one of the indicators of heroism. We often don't look at it like that, but it's part of the definition. As we get older we look back at choices and do the *what if*. I used to hate even considering to do a *what if* because to me, just doing it was admitting I might have made a mistake. But if we don't examine our past choices we will repeat bad ones.

Also, a danger is we can externalize and compare ourselves to our peers. I've got many classmates now retired or serving as gener-als in the army and I can *what if I had stayed in*, etc. etc. I did have a plan over 20 years ago and I threw it out the window over something that didn't work out. But as a sideways to that event, I ended up writ-ing. I think we can have goals and plan as much as possible, and then unexpected things happen.

A friend of mine always says when he hears *what if's* that if you were supposed to have done that, you'd have done it. Sounds simple, but it has a ring of truth to it. If I was supposed to have become a general, I'd have become a general. I'd have made all the choices to do it because I wanted it. Apparently I didn't want it because I didn't make those choices.

One thing writers tend to do is not tell people they are writers. I tell people I'm an author and they'll ask my name and say they never heard of me. If I'm feeling particularly snarky, I'll ask their name and say I never heard of them either. There isn't much validation in the world of publishing other than what we give ourselves.

"Have no fear of perfection—you'll never reach it." Dali

Our parent's voice in our head can be devastating or inspiring. Depending on the parents. It would be nice to think we can live in a vacuum and accomplish everything we want on our own, but some support is always good.

Those sayings from childhood are like weeds. Hard to pull them out. Writing them down, posting them somewhere so you remember that they are holding you back and then consciously ignore them might help. I've written down bad habits I have and posted it so I can remind myself and stop myself when I start to slip into them.

My theory is that a lot of people choose a career path for the wrong reasons. A lot of doctors and lawyers and business owners made the decision to do those things out of fear. I know a guy who was a very successful lawyer, woke up one day, and realized if he didn't go for his dream of being a writer *now*, he never would. He quit his high-paying job and committed to it. And it worked.

No more could've and should've. It's done.

A mentor is important. That is why so many keynote speakers at writers conferences tell their stories of how hard it was and how discouraged they got at times. They want to let you know that what you're going through is normal.

When I wrote military fiction I tried to avoid what I call the James Bond syndrome. Where the hero is handsome, skilled in every weapon, a martial arts expert, a gourmet chef, speaks six languages, a superb lover, can fly a plane/helicopter/spaceship—one who can do everything. Doesn't exist. In Spec Ops we had shooters. AKA guys who were great shots. They were unbelievably good at that. But that's all they did, every single day. They shoot. And became good at it. You can become good at what you choose to focus on.

To become stronger, what we did in training was put people in situations that seemed impossible. We did some lose-lose training (aka the *Kobyashu Maru* type thing from *Star Trek*) just to see how people thought and reacted. We also set very high standards. Standards that seemed out of reach, but then we helped and cajoled and coached people to meet and exceed those standards.

A flip side to that is you can become rather blasé about it. I was telling my wife about HALO parachuting. Then she saw a TV special about it and she told me what I told her in no way equaled what she watched on that show. I'd made it seem matter of fact and part of our normal job, which it was. But our normal job was not most people's normal job.

So think about things in your life that you consider matter-of-fact that to other people might be very scary. I was talking with a woman the other week who was taking her first trip to New York City and she was terrified. I grew up in NYC, so NY doesn't scare me. But put me in the middle of a square dance in a farming community and it's a different story.

They say one of the greatest fears is public speaking. I've been diagnosed with social anxiety disorder, but can give a keynote to five hundred people without a problem. A large part of it is feeling comfortable with the subject matter. On the other hand, standing with four people making 'small talk' is very, very uncomfortable.

We dealt with fear a lot in Special Operations, because even our training exercises could easily turn deadly. It is not normal to jump out of a perfectly good airplane at night, at 500 feet, with 150 pounds of rucksack, 42 pounds of parachute, and 30 pounds of weapon and combat vest. And that's just the start of the mission. But the more we faced our fear, the less power it had.

Living with fear is ultimately worse than confronting it. So what you must do sometimes is…

Attack The Ambush

My patrol is walking along a trail and suddenly we are fired upon from the right. My fear wants me to jump in the convenient ditch to the left—to avoid. The problem is, if the ambush is set up correctly—that ditch is mined and I'll die if I do that. My next fear-driven instinct is to just hit the ground. Stay where I'm at and do nothing. Except I'm in the kill zone and if I stay there, well, I'll get killed. The third thing I want to do is run forward or back on the trail to get out of the kill zone—escape. Except, if the ambush is done right, the heaviest weapons are firing on either end of the kill zone. And I'll die.

The correct solution is the hardest choice because it requires courage. I must conquer my fear, turn right and assault into the ambushing force. It is the best way to not only survive, but win.

There's the old saying for writers to 'write what they know'. However, maybe some of us need to write what we are *afraid* to know or face. I see many writers who avoid writing what they should be writing because it would mean confronting their fears. Be curious about your fear—it's a cave, but instead of a monster lurking inside there is treasure instead.

Remember fear is an emotion. Action can occur even when your emotions are fighting it. Taking action is the key to conquering fear. We expand our comfort zone by venturing into our courage zone.

Another way to conquer ours fears is by doing things we dislike, but need to do. If you're introverted, talk to a stranger every day. When I go to conferences I make sure I engage at least one stranger in conversation. I don't like doing it, but I know I need to.

If you're a practical person, do something intuitive every day.

Basically, do the exact opposite of your Myers-Briggs character and slowly you will find yourself stepping outside your comfort zone on a regular basis and achieving your goals. And your comfort zone is expanding.

Common Fears Of Writers

You have to be honest with yourself (and your shrink) in order to correctly identify your fears. The first step is to rip away the denial. If you say you have no fear, besides being in a Nike commercial, if you are being honest, then you are either a sociopath or a psychopath.

One thing to do is look at what you think is your greatest strength and turn it around. Why are you good at that? What is that strength compensating for that you lack or are afraid of?

Most fear is subconscious. You will likely need help finding the true root. So, yes, you will probably have to go to therapy. At the very least, you have to open yourself up to listening to what those around you think about you and honestly evaluate what they say.

In many cases we bend our lives around our fears. If you examine the way many people live, most major decisions they make are fear based. We might phrase it differently, "I want security" so I will stay at a job I hate for 30 years trying to get a retirement that might get wiped out in one day. We'll stay in relationships that make us miserable because the misery we know is easier to live with than the uncertainty of the unknown. We don't submit because "it's not ready yet", when the real reason is we don't want to be rejected.

Also, your fear won't change things. It has no power other than keeping you from taking positive action. I know people who, when they are afraid of something, make that fear almost a mantra. They believe by using that mantra, they keep the fear from coming true. If they are afraid of flying, they believe if they are terrified through the flight that is what is keeping the plane in the air.

Fear can become a self-fulfilling prophecy. In many businesses, the atmosphere of fear is destroying the business. Fearful people are less productive people.

Over the course of many years and many blogs on the topic of fear, I have compiled a list of the most common fears, concerns and questions writers have. I have put them below and answered them. Many of you will have the same fears. Many will have different fears. If I have not addressed your specific fears, feel free to email me at admin@whodareswinspublishing.com and I will be more than happy to add them to the list inside this book.

Fears

I'm Afraid I'm Writing To Get Validation From Families And Friends.

I think you're writing for your own validation. It would be nice if others gave some support. A problem with publishing is that an author, even when published, falls into what I call the 'black hole' where you hear nothing about anything for months at a time. You feel like you've disappeared off the face of the planet. I think that's why we have to dig deeper and also keep our focus on the strategic goal we want to achieve.

I don't think the word is validation. We want support from family and friends. Which is difficult when writing seems like such a nebulous thing to outsiders. I think setting and achieving specific supporting goals can help.

What I Fear Most Is Failure.

I'm not so sure I fear failure as much as I fear making a mistake that leads to failure. There is a big difference between the two. Also, because I fear making a mistake, that keeps me from making decisions.

I believe sometimes we have to look for the fear behind the fear. On the surface we think we're afraid of something, but if we delve deeper we find a different fear, that the surface fear is guarding.

I Fear Messing Up After I Succeed

That's putting the cart before the horse. Get the succeeding part down first.

Also, these nine Forces are not linear. They're circular. So if you succeed at achieving your strategic goal, you take a break, do an After Action Review (AAR) and start over again, just at a higher level. What do you want to achieve next? Then develop an entirely new plan, taking into account this particular fear. But having this fear before the success will probably keep you from the success. I think it's a very valid fear and a good point.

Once I Achieve Success It Will Dry Up

Get the success first, *then* worry about that. Plus, every published author I know is scared they can't do the next book. But it's a false fear in a lot of ways, because if you've achieved success with a book, and you learned so much writing that book, why shouldn't your second book be better? You have to get across the desert from one oasis to the next. But leaving one oasis behind and having it disappear over the horizon behind you can be a frightening experience if you're not quite sure where the next one is going to be. There's going to be a strong pull to turn around and go back to the known, rather than venture forward to the unknown.

Fear Of Being Alone

I translate that to fear of not being understood. There's a niche out there for everyone. With our writing we can find our niche, explore it, grow in it, and expand. Mention any title in a room full of people and some will love it, some will hate it, and many won't care.

You also need a network of writers. While I'm not the greatest fan of critique groups, I think it's essential that writers have other writers in their lives. And not just for the business networking, but more importantly, for the creative networking. When two writers are discussing a book they've read or a movie they've seen, their conversation is at a level most other people can't comprehend.

Rejections Where Editors Didn't Read—External Validation And Feeling Alone

This feeling alone thing is interesting. It can be very frustrating to not be understood. I think one needs a few solid people in their life who understand them, whether or not they are writers doesn't matter at a personal level. Professionally, though, you need writer friends. Because only a writer truly understands another writer. I think this is a problem a lot of editors and agents have. They don't understand our mindset.

Editors and agents don't really read. They don't have time. That's frustrating but reality. Even my editor at St. Martins Press who is quite brilliant—I can tell when we get the edited mess back from her that she hasn't read carefully because she'll ask questions that are clearly answered in the book.

This is why the great idea to hook is so important.

Fear Of Harsh Judgment Of My Work

Someone, somewhere won't like it and will tell you so. The first person you really have to please is yourself. Is it the best you can possibly make it? That's the main standard you have to pass before any external one.

We'll discuss critique groups later, but I think one has to be wary of a lot of those groups. I've actually seen groups tear down the best writers in the group. People aren't doing it consciously, but rather subconsciously out of the threat and jealousy of the better writer.

You've got to send it out there. It's part of the job description. Don't worry, after about five or ten years, you'll stop worrying about it, because your comfort zone will be so much larger with this. I hardly even think about things I send out now. I focus on what I'm currently working on. But I do remember ten years ago rushing in the door every day to check to see if the answering machine light was blinking. Now I fughedaboutit as we say in da Bronx, because I have no control of anyone other than me.

Fear Of Success

Yes, fear of success is very prevalent. It doesn't get any easier, but you get better at your craft. You have to build confidence in your abilities. But everyone has those waking up at 3 in the morning panic attacks where you think everything is screwed up and not going to work.

At Who Dares Wins, our sales have exploded this year. Secretly, we'd be thrilled if they just remained level, although we're constantly working to increase the numbers. But we also have a dread that one day we'll wake up and it will all be a mirage. That the success will have just disappeared.

Perseverance is the key to success.

Getting Tired Of Writing Or Not Making Enough Money To Keep Doing It

We all get tired of writing, especially when it becomes our day job. It can be a grind at times. When it's your main source of income you have to get up every day and get to work, regardless of how you feel. That was why that professor who said, "write what you feel" kind of ticked me off. No one cares how you feel. They care what you write. And if it's your job, you've got to do it regardless of how you feel. We have to remember, he was not making his living writing, he was making his living teaching. Writing was almost a sideline for him so he could afford to write what he felt.

I didn't go to the Naval Academy because I didn't know how to swim. The first day at West Point, they issued me a bathing suit along with all my other gear. I took that as a bad sign. I learned to survival swim. Then I reported to 10th Special Forces Group after training. My commander told me I was taking a Maritime Operations Team (operating with a focus on water missions) and our first deployment was to the Royal Danish Navy Frogman School. I told him I really didn't like the water. He told me he really didn't care what I liked or didn't like, I was going. I look at writing the same way. There are days I really don't want to do it, but I do it anyway. And the result is pretty much the same.

Not making enough to keep doing it: Frankly, I think that's the number one reason writers are concerned about money. We love writing so much, we just want to make enough to keep going. What's great about indie publishing is I now get several paychecks at the end of every month and I know exactly how much they will be. I know how many books I have to sell in order to make enough to sustain myself every month. It's no longer a great mystery. This is motivating after so many years in traditional publishing.

That I Might Be A Bad Writer And Not Realize It

It's a craft. It can be learned. I've seen writers make tremendous strides when they focus on learning the craft. Don't concern yourself with worry about being a bad writer, concern yourself with learning to be a better writer. There's a big difference in focus between the two.

I also find it's a left brain, right brain thing. One day I look at my writing and think it's pretty good (right brain day), the next day, it's crap (left brain day). But regardless of what I feel, the writing is the same.

Fear Of Apathy Among Readers

I have a fear of apathy in any aspect of my life. I would rather have anger, than apathy. However, publishing is a business where external feedback is limited and not often a real representation. When we have apathy in our writing we will have apathy in our readers. Where we have passion in our writing, it will shine through to our readers.

That I Don't Have What It Takes To Realize My Dream

No one can tell you no. They can reject your manuscript, but they can't tell you no. The only person who can tell you no, is you. Take it out of the dream state and put it in the goal state. You want to be a published author? Then write it down and start aligning all your supporting goals to help you achieve that goal.

There once was a young man who had been playing the violin since he could first pick one up. He dreamed of being a concert violinist. One day, the great master who he respected came to his town for a concert. After the concert, the young man met the master and told him of his dream. The master asked the young man to play something.

The young man played his heart out.

When he was done, the master was silent for a few moments, then shrugged and said: "Not enough fire."

Then walked out.

The young man was crushed. He put his violin away and never played again. He went into another career. Years later the master came back to town for a concert. The man met the master at a party and reminded him of that audition so many years ago and how it had crushed him.

The master was surprised for a moment, then shrugged. "I tell everyone that. If what I said was enough to stop you, you truly didn't have enough fire."

That I'll Never Sell A Book

I might never sell another either. But selling is actually out of my hands to a large extent. What is in my hands is writing the best damn book I can. In fact, my attitude is to write a book they can't not buy. When we focus on negative it affects everything we do. Focus on what you can control and in today's publishing environment the writer controls a lot more than in the past. You have the opportunity to get your books to your potential readers.

Once I wrapped my brain around the idea that no matter what I do, either traditionally publish or self-publish, my work will be read by my readers, I was able to let this fear go completely.

Worried About Last Third Of Book, Pulling It Together Into A Happy Ending.

Are you writing the right genre? Frankly, I'm not a fan of the HEA—happily ever after. I watched the end of *Officer & A Gentleman* and was like, *Oh yeah, that's gonna last.*

So I think maybe look at this two ways. First, maybe you want to write a different book than one that has a HEA? Or second, maybe you need to suspend your own disbelief as an author a bit more to give yourself the freedom to write this type of book?

Frankly, this was a problem in my career as a military thriller writer and one reason I did not go back to that was my endings were not HEA. Yes, the good guys defeated the bad guys, but outside of that particular conflict the world did not change. There were still bad guys out there. And it almost seemed a lot of waste went on.

Fears In General

We think we are the only one who has all these fears, then to find out we all share them is a relief. That's a key to networking and really talking with other writers.

Writing fears down makes them real. It's scary but making them real, means they are real obstacles that can be overcome.

Some people say you should laugh in the face of fear. Laughter is a good thing, but always laughing everything off, not necessarily, because that could just be a defense against real things. It is good to wear life loosely, but as a writer sometimes we have to really dig in and bleed. Plus, sometimes fear might laugh back at us.

The ability to adjust and adapt is a key tenet of Special Forces. I mentioned that what made us elite was our detailed and intensive planning. But as we said in the Infantry, *the plan works up until you cross the line of departure/line of contact. That is until you engage the enemy, because they have their own plan.*

Life has its own plan too. So no matter how good your plan is, it's going to change. But it's always better to have a good plan as the base to change off of, than constantly reinventing everything all the time.

Saying I Can't Is Really Saying I Won't.

I also think a degree of risk-taking is important too. I go into this under the Rule-Breaking part later on, but I've always taken risks.

Yet I never gamble, unless I have control of the outcome. So what does that mean? It means that I have a deep-seated belief in my abilities, despite my fears. I also make a realistic appraisal of myself and see where I'm doing **I won't**. And try to change that to **I will.**

Courage, Communication and Fear

I believe that most people want to be the best they can be. I remember taking over a recon platoon in 1st Cavalry Division. They were labeled a poor unit and had just failed a major test. I did what I always did: walked in and told the men they already had my respect, they could only lose it, and I had to earn their respect. And I treated them that way. I let them do the jobs they'd been trained to, rather than micro-manage. And they came together. I think people tend to work and live up to higher expectations if they are respected. So self-respect is important to all of us who feel like frauds at times.

Integrity comes from being honest with one's self. Knowing the right thing. And doing it. If your fear is not being good enough, although you describe it in terms of how others will react to you, perhaps the blind spot is you're already treating yourself in the way you fear others will treat you, on a subconscious level.

Final Thought On Fear

We have to factor fear into our lives because we will always have something that we are afraid of. Fear is not inherently bad. It just is. The key to dealing with our fears is understanding what we are really afraid of, why we are afraid, and finding the best course of action to overcome our fears.

Fear is a motivator and an indicator. Don't discount fear, but don't let it rule your life and decision-making. If I had done that Who Dares Wins Publishing would have never existed.

Area Three: Dares

To **COMPLETE** the Circle of Success, to push yourself beyond the ordinary, you must master personal **COMMUNICATION** and **COMMAND** and then be daring enough to use everything you've learned, break rules & succeed.

"Great spirits have always found violent opposition from mediocre minds. The latter cannot understand it when a man does not thoughtlessly submit to hereditary prejudices but honestly and courageously uses his intelligence and fulfills the duty to express the results of his thoughts in clear form."

Albert Einstein

DARES—Problems

Not taking charge of your career will doom you. It's the biggest mistake I made early in my career. I expect other people such as my agent or editor to take control of my career. Only I know exactly what I want. My career is my responsibility and no one cares about it as much as I do.

Not communicating effectively beyond the manuscript will keep it from ever being seen. We spent a lot of time talking about goals. In my *Writer's Workshop* we spend a lot of time on book goals. In the beginning of *Write It Forward* we spent a lot of time focusing on your specific career strategic goal and your supporting goals. The manuscript is only one aspect of all your goals and it's important to communicate that outward.

Inability to pull all the parts of Write It Forward together for mission execution will waste effort. Your mission is to achieve your goals. A plan without action is nothing. I've seen many writers plan out their careers and then do nothing to achieve it other than writing it down. You must act.

Leadership is your responsibility. You are in the driver's seat. This is a critical component to being a successful author in the 21st century. Why? Because never before have there been so many viable options for writers. For twenty years I left leadership up to my agents and my publishers. For twenty years I was mildly successful. Then things changed in publishing and it was adapt or die. I adapted. But more importantly I also assumed personal leadership and started Who Dares Wins Publishing. It was both scary and freeing at the same time. The first person you have to lead is YOU.

You must have effective written and oral communication skills. The old maxi think before you speak fits nicely here. The key to effective communication is to take the point of view of the person receiving the message.

You must understand your creative process in communicating. Every writer does things differently when creating a book. Every author runs their business differently. Everyone communicates differently.

You must pull together all aspects of Write It Forward for success. I have lived and used these techniques for more than three decades. They work.

Then you start over again from the beginning at a higher level. One of the things Jen Talty and I constantly do at Who Dares Wins Publishing is evaluate our business and hone the plan to achieve the next level.

Tool Seven: Communication

Communication is essential to success. It's how you interact with the world. It's a two way street—you must get your message across and receive true messages that others are trying to send you.

You must understand your creative process in communicating, where you are strong and where you need to improve.

The bottom line is that as writers, we are communicators.

Communication—The Problems

Most people don't know the true purpose of communication. They consider it only from their point-of-view, which is a mistake. When you communicate you must always look at how the receiver will take in the information you are sending. The goal of communication is to get the desired response.

Many people send subconscious negatives in their communication. Whenever you start off by saying, "I was wondering" or "I was hoping" it's actually sending a subconscious message to the receiver that you are not confident. Where you might think you are being polite, you are actually rejecting yourself.

Much of communication isn't codified. We'll discuss Standing Operating Procedures which make communication much more efficient and effective.

Communication—The Solutions

Understand the advantages and disadvantages of written communication. When you are communicating via email remember you are not sending non-verbal communication nor are you receiving non-verbals. This makes communicating effectively more difficult because all you have are the words on the page. However, written communication can be short and to the point, getting across only the specific message without any fillers. In places like Twitter, this can be quite a challenge. Always consider the medium of communication when deciphering a message.

Understand the advantages and disadvantages of oral communication. The main advantage of oral communication is the non-verbals given by each party. However, unless you know and understand non-verbals you could be misreading them.

Understand which form of communication is a strength for you and which one is a weakness. We are writers, so one would think that written communication is our strength. However, I can give keynote presentations to rooms in excess of over 500 people without a second thought and I'm very good at getting my message across. One on one, individual or small group conversations, are not my strong suit so I have to work harder in those situations.

Also, I'm good at writing my messages, but not so great at organizing my thoughts. That's why I had my business partner go through this manuscript and re-organize and re-structure because she's better at it than I am.

Learn how to use Standing Operating Procedures. I am a huge fan of SOPs. By writing out your own SOPs you are communicating to yourself an expectation and a set of rules. When you write out SOPs for your business, you are making yourself and those around you accountable. At Who Dares Wins Publishing we have checklists and while each of us has different responsibilities, we constantly check each other. If Jen didn't write out her SOPs for formatting a book, I wouldn't be able to check her and vice versa.

Understand your creative process in communicating. Simply stated, understand how your brain forms ideas and how your brain interprets ideas. Are you a big picture person? Or are you detail oriented? Do you outline and plan? Or do you write by the seat of your pants? How you outline your day is how you will outline your book. The same is true for how you communicate.

What Is Communication?

The primary goal of communication is to evoke a response. Thus the receiver of the communiqué is more important than the sender. Therefore, the sender needs to take the point of view of the person the message is intended for.

When we communicate, we are transmitting both logic and emotion. We are also transmitting on the conscious and subconscious levels. We are externalizing something internal. All four must send the same message.

Receiving a message correctly is also key. Figuring out what someone is really trying to transmit is a critical skill. This is the infamous *read between the lines* whether it be written, oral or action communication. When I speak with agents and editors, I usually have to *translate* what they are really saying. This is because they view manuscripts and the business with a different point of view than a writer. Often they can say something is wrong with a manuscript and kind of sort of say what it is, but often they can't pin it down. The reason is two-fold. They are not writers and it's not their manuscript.

The Role Of Fear In Communication

Fear can make people dishonest, both consciously, and more often subconsciously. If something in a message disturbs you, focus on it. Sometimes you are disturbed because the *words and the music* aren't in sync. What that means is that what someone is saying doesn't equal what they are doing and what they mean.

Laziness can also make people deceptive. I had an agent fail to do what he said he was going to simply because he didn't want to take the time and effort. Those of you who are published have probably heard the refrain from editors and publicists on how they are going to work hard on your books and give you tons of effort in publicity, but when the pub date comes, the efforts rarely equal the words. They aren't lying, and they have the best intentions, they are just overwhelmed. Also, my experience has been they just flat out don't want to tell you the reality, "we're sending out galleys to the usual suspects and that's pretty much it." If they do that much.

Action is the primary and most reliable means of communication.

Want to know if an agent is legitimate or not? They should give you a list of recent sales or referrals to existing clients. I get emails from friends who say they are talking to an agent who won't tell them sales or give at least one referral and I find that odd. It's a business relationship. If they don't trust you, why should you work with them?

In the same way, your actions are going to make the greatest impression with other people. Do you deliver your manuscripts on time? Do you do all you can to promote your books? Are you professional on social media and don't get bogged down in arguments, political and religious stances, etc. When you do book signings do you treat readers with the respect they deserve as consumers of your product? Do you respond promptly to emails?

The first thing I do when an author queries Who Dares Wins Publishing is Google the author. What does your social media presence say about you? Do you even have one? What does your blog say about you? If you spend your blog complaining about publishing and how stupid editors and agents are, don't you think an editor or agent considering your work is going to read that? Anything you put out there in electronic form is there forever.

When you go to conferences, do you present yourself well? My business includes more than just writing, but also consulting and speaking. People outside the writing world have different standards. Therefore I dress up more than I used to when I go to conferences. First impressions are important.

Beware Of The Subconscious Negative

Because you are also transmitting on the subconscious level, you have to focus very hard to make sure that level supports your conscious level. If you have the time, never respond immediately in writing (a danger of email). Watch your word choice. This also applies in your manuscript. I never have a character in my manuscript yawn or become bored. The second a character does it, the reader does it.

For example, after finishing a manuscript, aspiring novelists have to write query/cover letters, which is similar to a resume for the book and the writer. These are sent to agents and editors, as authors begin the long road toward trying to get published. When I teach, I spend a lot of time on the cover letter, pointing out common mistakes, one of which is the subconscious negative. These are words or sentences that reflect negatively on the writer or the book. Starting a query letter with the phrase, *I hope you like the book*, for example, is a subconscious negative. It indicates fear and uncertainty, because you're telling the person you're not exactly sure they're going to like it and don't have confidence in what you've done. On your query, never say anything negative about yourself or your manuscript. Remember, we teach people how to treat us. I've seen many authors say negative things about themselves on their cover letters, sometimes using self-deprecation as a social strategy. When you put that out in the world it's magnified and comes back to you negatively.

Often, query letters bad-mouth the very business the writers is trying to get into, by making comments about how difficult it is to get published and the lack of acumen on agents and editors' parts to see the author's brilliance.

In the opposite direction, a subconscious negative is putting the copyright symbol on the cover sheet for the manuscript. It's intimating, *I think this is so good, I'm afraid you're going to steal it.* Uh, no.

Another subconscious negative I focus on is the, *we'll see*. Any time you say that phrase really focus on what you're doing. *We'll see* comes from:

- *Nurture (lack of)*
- *Desire to protect oneself*
- *Not saying "I'll see". Separates yourself from your goal*
- *FEAR*

Written Communication

Writing makes things real. That is the main reason I keep saying, "write it down". I have great thoughts and ideas and visions in my head, but having to actually write them down often brings them down a notch. Remember, our occupation is writer, not thinker, even though most of our work day is sitting at our desk staring at the ceiling with a bit of drool coming out of our mouth.

We speak differently than we write. Read a court transcript to see that. Often they don't make sense because you have none of the non-verbals in the oral communication that is being recorded. Also, beware of slang and abbreviations—people are often afraid to ask for clarification.

Think Like The Reader

When communicating, think like the receiver.

When I write, I always take the reader's point of view into account. This is both when I'm writing a book and when I'm writing a communication to another person. Am I going to get the reaction I desire? Always take the point of view of the receiver of the communiqué.

I've heard it said that writing is the only art form that isn't sensual. If you think about it, the printed page affects the senses the same way. Music doesn't. Paintings don't. We could argue the point, but writing really limits you in that you are trying to get something from inside your head, into the head of the reader, through the sole medium of the printed word. This is one reason some of the hardest writing is humor. You're the standup comic without the stand up.

Writing signifies responsibility. You wrote it, you own it. This is one thing to consider with the internet. Anything you put out there in the public domain is there forever for anyone to see.

Don't qualify, say what you mean and say it simply. If you're writing someone and you say, "I think . . ." what does that mean? Aren't you thinking it just because you're writing it? If you write, *It seems as if . . .* Well, is it or isn't it?

EXERCISE: What genre are you writing in? What point of view do you write in?

The genre/type of book you write most likely reflects the genre/type of book you like to read. Every genre has some slightly different things about it. Over the years I've seen certain trends among writers of certain genres. For example, fantasy writers world build. And they can get so caught up in the world building they forget the reader has no clue.

Science fiction writers like inventing neat things. But sometimes they put so many neat things into their story it overwhelms the main plot line. Then, instead of getting rid of some of the neat things that aren't important, they just swap them around like deck chairs on the *Titanic.*

Thriller writers love action, to the point where their characters can become cardboard cutouts moved around as needed for action. Mystery writers like dialogue to the point where there can be no action. I am starting to see certain types of writers get attracted to certain genres. The problem a lot of fantasy writers have is they have spent so much time building this world and universe, that they are very familiar with it. They forget the reader hasn't a clue who Princess Xgrths is, and why the Kingdom of Posaawd is fighting the Kingdom of Kllasw for control of the infamous Ewqfcmee, whatever the heck it is.

The point of view you write in, most likely reflects the point of view you like to read. I've always had a problem with point of view. I've written in every one: 1st, 2nd, 3rd limited and omniscient. Finally, I spent a weekend reading a bunch of my favorite books and the Moment of Enlightenment came. The authors I enjoyed reading almost all wrote in omniscient.

As you can see, point of view can make or break the communication in your novel. When communicating with others in written and oral communication it's important to understand your own point of view as well as the point of view of the intended receiver in order for the communication to be effective and fully understood.

EXERCISE: Do you outline? Or do you just write and then rewrite?
EXERCISE: What are you better at: plotting or character?

The Creative Process And Communication

How do you organize your daily life? This is how you will organize/ outline your book. It is also how you will communicate to those around you. The good news is, if your organizing skills in daily life aren't that great, you can always work on them, especially with regard to your book.

If you outline, do you outline just plot, or do you outline characters? Or do you do both? I recommend putting most of your effort into the part you're weakest in. For example, if you're very good at plot, spend a lot of time on your characters before you start writing the manuscript. Consider front-loading the part of the book that is your weakest writing. Your tendency is going to be to want to do the work in the area you're strongest in. You have to fight that tendency and really focus on building up the weakest part of your skill set.

If you're a pantser, how much rewriting do you do? I submit to you that everyone outlines. For the pantser, their outline is called the first draft.

Is your rewriting focused on plot or character? I have several layers to rewriting now. I pull different characters and just look at their scenes in their entirety to make sure the characters and dialogue are consistent and the characters have arc. I rewrite for symbol consistency. I rewrite for theme consistency. I rewrite for fact consistency. I rewrite for timeline consistency.

Consider genre in terms of your strengths & weaknesses as a writer. I'm writing historical now because it's my passion, but also because it allows me to focus on character because the timeline of the book is set. The energy I used to devote to plot in my thrillers now goes into character development in my historical fiction.

If you are an introvert, how do you write other people? We talked about character earlier, but it is my take that a lot of writers use real people (somewhat changed) in their books.

What anomaly does your main character have? I always go back to this word in my workshops. I had an agent look at story ideas I sent him and he basically said: I get 50 of these a week. Give me a character dossier. Read *Day of the Jackal* and give me a character like that.

What you want is some aspect to your protagonist that doesn't seem to fit. You know the reason for this anomaly, but the reader doesn't. That draws the reader in. Give the protagonist a trait that doesn't seem to fit his character: I like using the movie *LA Confidential*. In it, the protagonist, Russell Crowe, is a brute cop. He's used as muscle. No one thinks he's very bright. But he has this weird streak in him that he will always help a woman in peril. The movie opens with that. And it defines his character arc. He even explains far into the movie why he has that trait. I really recommend the movie. Extremely well written. And the Rollo Tomasi technique is brilliant.

The raw materials of your life are the essence for your writing. If you get blocked or frustrated while writing, consider writing a scene where a character is blocked or frustrated. Often, we figure things out by writing. You can always throw it out. But a blank page isn't helpful.

Remember, successful writing is entertaining writing.

Standing Operating Procedures Codify And Help Change Habits

Standing Operating Procedures are anything written down that delineates how things should be done and to give guidelines. They can serve many purposes. The key part of the first sentence of this paragraph is *written down*. Once more, writing something down makes it real. It also makes it easily available to all. It reduces confusion and misunderstanding. It reminds you of lessons learned and keeps you from making the same mistakes over and over.

Every job I've ever done, I've ended up writing an SOP for it. Usually I do this because, surprisingly to me, no one before me did that, even when it was part of their job. I also did it so I could better understand what I was supposed to be doing. Have you ever spent hours figuring out how to do something, then a few months later go back to repeat the same action, but you can't remember how to do it? SOPs come in handy when either teaching someone else your job, or when it's a task that is not performed on a daily basis, yet has specific steps that must be taken or the task will not be completed properly.

While it takes time to write down your SOPs, in the long run it will save you a lot of time and headaches.

When I finished my Special Forces training at Fort Bragg, I was issued orders assigning me to the 10th Special Forces Group (Airborne) at Ft Devens, MA. As one of the last of the 1st Lieutenant Executive Officers to serve in SF, I was assigned to ODA 054 as the team's executive officer. After being in-briefed by the team leader, he asked me if I had any questions. The first thing I did was ask him for a copy of the team's SOP, as I had been taught to do at Fort Bragg. I was surprised when he told me they didn't have a written one. He had explanations why they didn't need one, but ultimately, in retrospect, the primary reason was no one had taken the initiative to write one, because writing an SOP is a very time consuming process. It's a 'front-end'-'back-end' deal. You put the work in on the front end to save you considerably more time in the long run on the back end. Unfortunately, too often, people are overwhelmed up front and don't see the larger and long range picture.

When I took command of my own A-Team a few months later, once again, the first thing I asked was where was the team SOP. After my previous experience, I wasn't too surprised when I was told the team didn't have one written down. They *knew* what they needed to do, I was told. Right. And even if they did, how was I supposed to *know* it?

That was my first experience with computers as I bought one of the first Mac computers—no hard drive, switching disks, black and white screen—and began writing the team SOP. Basically, I began formalizing what everyone said they *knew*. I not only drew from my team members' expertise, I went to other teams and found those who did have SOPs and got copies. I went to the company headquarters and talked to the Sergeant Major who had extensive combat experience and got him to help, giving us small tips—seemingly small, but ones that could save your life in combat.

When completed, the team SOP was rather detailed. The beginning of it was my policy letters, spelling out our philosophy for leading the team as well as my team sergeant's letters.

My team sergeant, as was his way, was direct and to the point. Here were some of his choicer lines.

- *Nothing is impossible to the man who doesn't have to do it*
- *Smith & Wesson beats four aces*
- *The latest information hasn't been put out yet*
- *There are two types of soldiers– the steely eyed killer and the beady-eyed minion*
- *They give these people guns*

Here are some excerpts from mine.

- *Most basic tenet of teamwork is honesty*
- *With rank & privilege comes responsibility*
- *Everyone is a leader*
- *We do everything together*
- *Don't get in a pissing contest with a man on a balcony. You just end up wet and smelling. If you have a problem with someone above us, let me know*
- *Keep a positive attitude*
- *Discipline stays at team level*
- *Be on time*
- *Keep your sense of humor. You'll need it*

After the policy letters, we then specified who on the team was responsible for what. We took much of this from the field manual for Special Forces that had this information. Again, as mentioned earlier, you can help yourself tremendously when writing an SOP for yourself to check out what is already out there. Someone, somewhere, probably wrote one just like what you want to write.

When I was first published I attended a continuing education class on magazine writing. I didn't have a plan to write articles, but I figured it was a form of writing so I would learn something. I was trying to get out of the trap of tunnel vision. The instructor gave out a thin comb-bound booklet covering the material he was going to teach. I thought this was a good idea and when I was getting ready to teach my first writing class, I did the same.

My first draft of what I called *The Fiction Writer's Toolkit: A Guide To Writing Novels and Getting Published* was eleven pages long. That's how much I consciously knew about the subject matter, even though I'd already had three books published. As the years progressed and I wrote more books and taught more, I would continuously update the Toolkit. After eight years it became over ninety-thousand words long and was eventually published by Writer's Digest as *The Novel Writer's Toolkit: A Guide To Writing Great Fiction and Getting It Published* and was just rewritten and updated last week and published by my own company as *The Novel Writers Toolkit*. Does that mean I learned so much new stuff over the years? Yes, but what I also did was begin to move things I *knew* from my subconscious to my conscious. There was no way I would have published three books if all I knew was eleven pages worth of material about writing. An SOP is an excellent way to formalize things you already know, but aren't quite sure that you know.

Special Operations has always relied on SOPs. If you get a copy of the current US Army Ranger Handbook, which every good Infantry and Special Forces officer should be packing, in the very beginning is a list of Roger's Rules of Rangering. The first Rangers were formed in 1756 and Rogers wrote his rules in 1759 after three years of combat experience on the frontier. Some of these sound quite simple but they were learned at the cost of blood.

- *Don't forget nothing*
- *Tell the truth about what you see and do*
- *When you're on the march, act the way you would if you were sneaking up on a deer. See the enemy first*

- *Don't never take a chance you don't have to*
- *When we camp, half the party stays awake while the other half sleeps*
- *Don't ever march home the same way. Take a different route so you won't be ambushed*

And so on—all very basic, but rules that are constantly violated every day by military forces.

Whatever your job is, you should have an SOP for it. And it should be written so that someone with no background can achieve a base level of functioning in the job for a short period of time. Other SOPs should lay out the way your organization works. The way things really work, not how you want someone to think they work.

Failure to follow SOPs lays the groundwork for disaster, as is failing to study history.

For writers, some SOPs you should have are:

- A social media SOP (covering Twitter, Facebook, Kindle-boards, etc.)
- A blind spot SOP which lists bad habits and is posted where you can easily see it every day in order to keep from indulging in your bad habits
- A process SOP where you sketch out your creative process for writing a book
- A travel SOP where you have a packing list for conferences along with a checklist for vital material such as passport, plane tickets, reservations, etc.
- A blog SOP so you do all the little things needed when posting a blog such as tags, timeliness, etc.

SOPs should be followed, but also evaluated in the face of changing circumstances. SOPs are not written in stone. SOPs need to be checked every once in a while to make sure that they are applicable and that they are being followed. Having a nice looking binder with wonderfully written SOPs does you no good if you don't read them or follow them. And SOPs that are out of date can cause more harm than good. They should be constantly updated based on After Action Reviews, which we will cover shortly.

An example of a Writing Standing Operating Procedure I use is a list in my office of my Blind Spots. Those things I have a tendency to do that have a negative effect. I use that list to remind me of character flaws I'm trying to overcome and often stops me from screwing up. Many of the exercises you've done in this course have given you answers that you can post and use as personal SOPs.

Here are some of mine.
- *Less is better*
- *Never respond right away in email*
- *Resist the temptation to engage editors & agents on twitter*
- *Slow down*
- *One thing at a time*
- *Decide*
- *WIP always first*

SOPs stop you from re-inventing the wheel. Take what you 'know' and write it down.

I just read an interesting article that said that hospitals that use pre-surgery and post-surgery checklists cut their mortality rates in half. Simple things like: Is this the right patient? Is this the right surgery for this patient? Is this the correct arm to amputate? Have we accounted for all our equipment after the surgery?

We had strict checklists for being a Jumpmaster. In fact, in my JM class, 14 of 85 students graduated. Because you had to score 100% on every single test. There is no 99% when jumping out of an airplane.

One time my team borrowed some old, beat up shotguns from the military police and went out to the range to blast some rounds, because we had an overstock of shotgun rounds. So we fired all day. The range checklist said we had to account for every single expended shotgun round. It was a Friday, it was late, and everyone was like *screw it, no big deal, the guys at the ammo point aren't going to count them either.* But because it was the SOP I made us do it and we ended up one round short. We went on the truck and checked the shotguns and sure enough, one had a round in the chamber. Someone could have died if we had not followed the SOP.

It's not just the checklist—it's the added focus. There's a thing called the Hawthorne effect, which is that by simply observing something, you change the something, usually for the better. I used the example of checklists in hospitals cutting mortality rates by 50%. But it wasn't just the checklists it was the fact that the people operating knew they were being observed during a test to see if the checklists worked, that improved things. In writing, I think something like #nanowrimo is an example of the Hawthorne effect. Or #writegoal on Twitter, where you're posting your progress out there for others to see.

Do you have a daily, weekly, monthly, checklist for your writing? And your blogging? And conferences? Do you keep track of your submissions and all your business correspondence?

War-Gaming Rules

War-gaming is my term for a critique group. Most of these rules or SOPs come from Susan Mallery (www.susanmallery.com) who has three other authors that she meets twice a year in Las Vegas to plot out two books each.

- *All sessions will be double-taped*
- *We will speak clearly and loudly so as to be heard on tapes*
- *We will not talk over anyone speaking*
- *We will all come with something about our story. Even just an idea*
- *The author of the hour is responsible for making sure she likes the direction we are going. If she does not, she needs to speak up ASAP*

- *Only the author of the hour controls the direction of the brain-storming*
- *No idea is bad. We will never be critical of someone's idea. If we don't agree, we can say something like: "Or you could try . . ."*
- *If the session is going badly, we will rewind tapes and start over. If still going badly, we will break and try again later*
- *We respect each other's ideas, meaning their ideas are theirs and theirs alone. However, if an author chooses not to use an idea, anyone interested in it may ask to use it*
- *All idle chitchat, gossip, confessions etc. are held in the highest degree of confidence. Anyone who violates this will not be asked back*

The rules are simple and clearly defined and keeps the group focused and on task. One of the things we will talk about in the *Write It Forward Critique Group Guide* is how most critique groups get derailed because the group doesn't have focus and they don't have a specific set of SOPs that the entire group is responsible for. Most of the individual critique groups are focused only on their needs and the way they do things which is fine when writing in isolation, but in order for a critique group to be successful, standardized rules are necessary.

This group also uses a checklist for plotting and character development so that each member will walk away with a template for their current work in progress.

Book Checklist
- *Hero's goal*
- *Hero's conflict*
- *Opening scene*
- *First TP*
- *Second TP*
- *Third TP*
- *Black moment*

- *Escalating bad stuff*
- *Scene stuff*

A key thing she does is record the war-gaming. I do that now in my *Write It Forward* workshops. In the past, an author would be so busy writing down the great ideas people were putting out, that they lost track of things or stopped participating.

Communication And Rejections

- It will happen. I estimate that for every one yes I have received, I averaged 49 no's
- Don't take it personally or react. Usually, there's no room at the inn
- In essence, in publishing, a rejection is primarily an emotional decision that someone then invents logical reasons for
- If you get a personal letter as a rejection that actually is a good thing. It means someone took the time to reply rather than send the usual form
- Use any feedback constructively
- Rejection is an emotional decision, then they invent logical reasons
- "We want something like X, but not X." is one of my favorite types of rejection
- Once the book is done, it's not your baby, it's a product

Things To Consider When Pitching/Communicating With An Agent/Editor

It is not an all or nothing thing. The odds of a pitch working are the same odds as getting pulled out of the slush pile. So view it more as a learning experience.

The content is key. No matter how great a salesperson you are, it always comes down to the idea and writing. Make sure you can clearly communicate the original idea of your book in a few sentences at most. Don't just sit down and lecture the agent or tell them the entire story. The goal is to get them to ask questions.

Know your *Write It Forward* strategic goal. Look past just the book you are pitching. You're thinking in terms of having a career as a writer.

Publishing is a business. I watched the guys from Amazon who presented last month in Seattle in their jeans and loose shirts and that's fine for Amazon, but I think first impressions are key. Over the years, I've found myself dressing more and more professionally as I go to conferences. There is an impression I want to make.

The pitch is not the end result. It's a path. Try to get feedback. You've paid for that person's time. Ask them questions. Ask them how they think you could improve what you're doing.

Never Complain, Never Explain

Is a rule I try to follow, not always successfully. Try to control your emotion. You cannot change other people's minds. It's very hard to let go sometimes, but you have to do it. Arguing with someone only gives them more things they can use against you and also makes them feel that their position is more valid.

When I critique manuscripts, I tend to ask a lot of questions. I always tell the writer that they shouldn't send back a letter with answers. I tell them they have to *explain* in the manuscript by rewriting. You don't get to stand in the aisle in the bookstore and explain what the reader doesn't get.

Marketing And Communication

Often times *Marketing*, *Promotion* and *Sales* get tossed around as if they are the same thing. They are not. There is a very good reason why the *Marketing Department* and the *Sales Department* are separate. *Promotion* is a part of marketing, but not all of marketing.

It is important for a writer to understand how all this plays into their career, especially in the current marketplace and it doesn't matter if you are *traditionally published* or *self-published,* you are going to have to have a *marketing plan* and understanding the basics is key to success.

Marketing is a set of activities and a process for creating and communicating something that will have value for customers. Marketing is a Strategy. It's the plan. It's the initial shift from production of a product to getting the product out there. When you market yourself and/or your book focus on the message you want to send and who you are sending the message too.

Promotion is one of the 4 p's in the Marketing Mix *(product, placement, promotion* and *price).* Promotion is a tool that supports your over all marketing plan and is intended to increase awareness. As an aside, some say there are 7 p's *(product, placement, promotion, price, physical environment, people, process).* Of course the marketing guru's say there is an 8th p and that is *Packaging.* We are going to focus on the sending the right message to the right people.

Sales is the act of selling a product or service in return for money or some other type of compensation. Most of the time, authors do NOT sell their books, with the exception of when they are hand-selling physical books at a conference or signing. I believe this is a key statement because even though you must always be promoting in every thing you do, you need not always be selling and there is a subtle difference.

There is an argument that Marketing can potentially negate the need for Sales. It's the idea that once great marketing and solid promotion are set into place it will bring more people *through the door.* If your promotional efforts have done their job effectively and the number of interactions between *product* (you and your book) and *consumer* (the reader) have increased then the consumer is already aware and willing to shell out the necessary dollars to get your book.

Marketing is a strategy AND one of your supporting goals. If your goal is to be a NY Times Best-Selling author, some of your fate is sealed by the size of the print run and marketing dollars that your publisher is giving you, but if you sit idle, then you've done nothing to maximize your potential. Whatever your publishing goals, marketing will play a large role. We will discuss more of this under **COMMAND**.

The field of Marketing encompasses everything a company does (writer/publisher) in the management of any given product (book). The biggest part of your marketing plan is WRITING YOUR BOOK.

When it comes to books, content is KING. PRODUCT rules. Your book has to be good to make it long term AND it has to be something the public desires and we all know how fickle consumers can be when it comes to books. The good news is that no matter what you are writing…there is a market for it…but you have to understand the consumers in that given market.

As a writer, you have to balance **Content** with **Promotion**. We will cover this later, but for now, understand that the most powerful marketing tool you have is your book. Your quality book is the foundation for any **marketing plan**. Writing the better book is the most important aspect of being a writer. Your marketing plan will grow organically out of that. The best promotion you can do is a good book, and better promotion is more books.

You **can market** your book, but you **can't sell** your book. The only book I've ever seen being successfully "sold" by **selling methods** is the Encyclopedia.

Think of marketing and promotion as sharing your excitement, not selling your book. Hook people with what excited you to write to begin with by being present in your own marketing plan.

So what is a marketing plan anyway?

It's a detailed strategic plan (SOP) that covers your specific strategies on how to develop your product, advertise your product, promote your product and ultimately end in a sale. In terms of an author, it will in part be determined whether you are self-published or published by traditional means. This is because as an independent author you can control much of the plan. If you are traditionally published, there is a lot you don't control.

Here are some basic considerations every author should include when doing a marketing plan.

- *What do I want to achieve with this plan*
  - *Hit NY Times Best-Seller list*
  - *Hit top 100 of my genre on Amazon*
  - *Be Number 1 in the paid Kindle store*
  - *Sell 20k books in a month*
- *Who is my target audience*
  - *What is my genre and who typically reads it*
- *How will I reach them*
  - *Social Media*
  - *Advertising*
  - *Networking*
  - *Community*
- *What is my message*
  - *What is my platform*
  - *Brand*
  - *Focused on series, Genre, Book*
- *What kind of promotion and advertising will I use*
  - *Can I offer free books*
  - *Paid placement ads*
- *What is my promotional/advertising budget*
  - *Consider income versus expenses*
- *How will I measure the success of my marketing plan*
  - *Based on goal*
- *How long will I implement this plan*
  - *Time frame*
  - *Phases and stages of the plan*
- *After action review*
  - *Assess time/cost versus results*
  - *What part will I keep*

- *What parts will I change*
- *What will be added to the next year's plan*

One of the hardest things for an author to do is to go between left-brain and right-brain activities. We tend to lean more towards the creative side—the writing. But we are also business people and all the writers we know that are the most successful are very smart business people. Often its not the most talented that succeed, but those who develop their talent and do those things they must in order to succeed. Perseverance and hard work count for a lot in this business.

Communicating Your Marketing To Your Audience

Social media is the hot thing. I keep seeing agents and editors telling prospective authors they have to build a social media platform. They want to know how many people are following you on twitter and how many people read your blog, etc. etc.

Frankly, most of it is BS, especially for fiction writers. I see so many people wasting time on twitter and blogs no one reads. My rule of thumb is write better books.

I'm not saying don't do it. But do it wisely. It's the content that is key. Like everything else, apply the Forces from this workshop:

What is your goal?

Are you informing, entertaining and networking?

Why are you doing it? I sense many people do it just so they can feel not alone in the world. Or that the fact 65,000 people are following them makes them feel better.

Where and when are you doing it? Are you spending all day there, or did you pick certain periods of time to do it?

I find social media much more helpful for my non-fiction and consulting. In fact, many people take my workshops because they heard about it on some form of social media.

Earlier we saw that INFJ= author and the opposite is ESTP= promoter. That's not saying you have to be an INFJ to be an author, but the trend is that authors tend to be pretty poor at 'selling' themselves.

Social media is a good way for writers to be 'social' because they can do it through their keyboard.

The trend also is publishers pushing more and more of the promotion for a book onto the author. That might lead one to ask what exactly do publishers do anymore? They distribute books, sure. But even that is going to go by the wayside. It's time for publishers to rethink their business paradigm, but right now, let's focus on us, the authors.

Some people view self-promotion as dirty. Yet, at the same time, if our book doesn't sell, we get upset and tend to blame others.

A hard lesson I've learned over the years, while content is important, it's not *all* important. Frankly, I've had thrillers published that were as good, if not better, than many on the bestseller list. I've read bestsellers that were poorly written. **Content** is still **King**, but **Promotion** is **Queen**. You need a combination of both. And even more so, you need to be consistent.

It's the same way I learned how to do better keynote talks. I used to focus on what I was going to say (content) and not so much on *how* I was going to say it. In fact, I used to say that motivational speakers were a waste. Yes, you felt good in the room but when you walked out, what did you really have in terms of useful content? The key thing I was missing was you felt good in the room and the speaker had your attention. There is something to be said for the moment and for the listener being engaged. I was too focused on the content and not focused on the receiver of the message. It goes back to point of view. And taking that a step further, I learned that if someone didn't buy a book now, they weren't going home and ordering it off Amazon. So the now is important.

So why do we writers have a hard time self-promoting?

- *We don't want to be considered arrogant*
- *We don't want to get confronted by people telling us we're self-promoting*
- *We're not sure what we're promoting is really worth it*
- *We don't want to be wrong*

The first key is, paradoxically, having good content. I started promoting my new publishing company, Who Dares Wins, by promoting my *Atlantis* books heavily. I'm following the #LOST on twitter and posting on it about the books. I have no problem doing that because there are numerous similarities between *Lost* and my books, and my books came out five years before the TV series. To the point, during the first season of *Lost*, I actually talked to a lawyer, believing I had been ripped off. Whether I had been or not (very hard to protect intellectual property), I know the books are good and will appeal to fans of *Lost*. I also know there are probably some people who hate seeing my posts on twitter. I try to keep it reasonable, but if I don't do it, who will?

Some of you have seen how reluctant I am to place my books out for sale when I'm presenting. That's an attitude I have to change, particularly now that I'm wearing two hats as author and publisher. One of our goals with Who Dares Wins Publishing is to create synergy among the brand by having our authors all promote. In fact, we're going to make that one of the selling points that makes us stand out from all the other publishers who can get a book up on kindle and other platforms. The future of publishing is changing and the days of sitting in a dark room, knocking out a book, and then expecting it to sell itself are over.

Sending A Message
- *Who is the target audience*
- *What desires/needs are you tapping into*
- *What message will touch those desires/needs*
- *Be consistent with message and brand*
- *Repeat the message again and again*
- *CONTENT, CONTENT, CONTENT*

Oral Communication
Is faster and more immediate than written. It is more situational than written communication as you often have to respond right

away. Remember that non-verbals are as large a part as the words spoken.

"I don't want any yes-men around me. I want everybody to tell me the truth, even if it costs them their jobs." Samuel Goldwyn.

Use oral communication to gather information and reduce misunderstanding. Use it for quick dissemination of information. Use it for goal-defining and goal/book planning.

Remember that when we listen to others, we filter everything through our point of view. Any emotional response, especially negative, is an indicator.

Something to consider about oral communication is to evaluate whom you are talking to and adjusting accordingly. We've covered differing points of view several times already. On top of that you need to get an idea of intellectual and experiential level the people you are talking to have.

Here is an example from my writing career. I was in Hollywood with Dan Curtis who had produced *The Winds of War* and *War and Remembrance*. He had optioned six of my books and produced a screenplay from one of them. We went over to Showtime to pitch this to a bunch of somebody's. All I know is that we went into a conference room and faced a handful of people, none of whom was over thirty. And they didn't ask any questions about the property we had come there to pitch.

One of them looked at me and gave me the classic, "Give me some ideas. What do you have?"

So I started throwing various story ideas on the table. Here was one, "What about a commando team that hides aboard Doolittle's bombers and jumps into Japan and—"

At that point the young man who had asked the question interrupted and asked: "Who's Doolittle?"

So scratch that pitch.

I'm not saying you have to dumb down, but you do have to be aware of who you are talking to.

Another example of not clearly understanding who you are talking to and making sure your oral instructions are understood is the case of Captain William Fetterman and Colonel Henry Carrington at Fort Phil Kearney in 1866.

Fort Kearney was established along the Bozeman Trail in Montana, right in the midst of traditional Sioux hunting grounds. Command of the Fort was given to Colonel Carrington who had no experience fighting Native Americans on the frontier and little command experience. In November of 1866 Captain Fetterman arrived at Fort Kearney. Fetterman had experience fighting along the frontier and held the belief that no force, no matter how large, of Native Americans could defeat a company of American soldiers. He claimed that he could ride through the entire Sioux nation with eighty men.

Carrington's command philosophy was to hunker down inside the Fort as much as possible. However, with winter approaching, a store of wood had to be put in. A wood train would go out from the Fort each day, having to range further and further as they depleted the nearby trees. Fetterman believed that the wood train was vulnerable to attack and pushed Carrington to launch a preemptive strike against the hostiles. Fetterman pressed the issue to the point where he was almost in outright rebellion against Carrington.

Sure enough, on 6 December, the various tribes in the area did attack the wood train. Carrington rushed forth with troops to rescue it. In the process he was attacked by a very large force of warriors and lost two men. Shaken, Carrington retreated and forbade his troops from chasing the enemy. The conflict between Fetterman and Carrington deepened.

Two weeks later, on 21 December, which happened to be the last day the wood train was going out, the Sioux again struck. Carrington was going to send one of his other captains to rescue the wood train and bring it back, but Fetterman stepped up and demanded the right to lead the rescue. A weak leader, Carrington yielded and gave command to Fetterman.

With seventy-nine men under his command—exactly equaling the eighty with which he had boasted he could ride through the Sioux nation—Fetterman prepared to leave the Fort. Carrington gave one last order before the column rode out the gate: *"Relieve the wood train. Under no circumstances pursue the enemy beyond Lodge Train Ridge."*

I've walked this battlefield and standing where the front gate of Ft. Kearney once was, immediately saw the reason Carrington gave this order, going beyond Lodge Train Ridge would take the relief column out of site of the remaining soldiers in the Fort.

As Fetterman's column approached the wood train, the Sioux who had been attacking it began to retreat. Naturally, given his temperament, Fetterman pursued. Just ahead of the troops, most of whom were Infantry (on foot) a small band of Sioux taunted them, still retreating. Leading that band was a young brave named Crazy Horse. Fetterman chased Crazy Horse and his small group up Lodge Train Ridge and to the consternation of the watching Colonel Carrington went over it and out of site.

Unknown to Fetterman and his command, the entire affair was a trap. Almost two thousand Sioux, Cheyenne and Arapahoe warriors were waiting in surrounding ravines, hidden out of site. As the soldiers continued to advance, a large party of warriors slid in behind them, cutting off their line of retreat to the Fort. The soldiers, armed with Civil War era muzzle loaders, tried to stand and fight, but the odds were so strongly against them the fight didn't last long, perhaps twenty minutes at best guess from those in the Fort based on how long they could hear firing before an ominous silence descended.

Fetterman and Captain Fred Brown saw the inevitable as the command was overwhelmed. They stood up, placed the muzzles of their pistols to the side of each other's head, counted, and fired simultaneously.

Eighty dead. It was the worst defeat for the army in the west and would remain so for ten years until a man named George Custer led the 7th Cavalry into the Little Big Horn, where a veteran of this battle, Crazy Horse, would meet him.

Carrington not only exercised poor leadership, his oral orders were pretty much worthless given Fetterman's character. Carrington should have never let Fetterman take command of the relief column or at the very least issued written orders that might have caused Fetterman a moment's pause in his brashness.

"Three may keep a secret, if two of them are dead." Benjamin Franklin.

A rule of thumb is **less is better**. That is for all forms of communication. I'm a fan of the one page synopsis which drives people crazy. The reason for that is I believe no agent is reading your synopsis unless you already hooked with the idea on your one page cover letter. So all you can do now is screw up. And the more stuff you put down, the more likely you will screw up.

When someone is arguing with you, the less you say, the better. In fact, if you examine the Miranda Warning it starts with "You have the right to remained silent." You know how many people do? Practically no one. Then it goes on to say, "anything you say can and will be used against you." It's like that in real life.

Importance Of Networking

People are more important than things. This point has been made over and over again throughout this book. We live and work among other people. A key technique that took me a while to understand was networking. At West Point and in the army, networking was pretty much forced upon me by the organization. I was in the same company at West Point for four years, enduring the same trials and tribulations as my classmates. In the Infantry we were a 'band of brothers' so to speak, and even more so on my Special Forces A-Team.

When I left the army, I moved to the Orient to study martial arts. I lived on the economy and was rather isolated. This was good because it allowed me to focus on what I was there to achieve, and also because it was where I began to write.

When I returned to the States, I had three completed manuscripts. I enrolled in graduate school as I continued to write and I also marketed those books. I got a three-book deal and my writing career began. Because the nature of being a writer was one of isolation, I did not have a network pressed upon me and I worked pretty much alone. I did not join a writer's group, nor did I attend events where other writers, editors, agents, etc. would be. This was a major mistake, one made partly out of ignorance, but also, honestly, out of foolish pride. I thought I could do it all on my own. I was wrong.

It took me years to see the error of my way. I gradually got out of my shell and went out of my way to meet people. I learned the importance of networking for the various reasons:

Emotional support. When we discuss Maslow's hierarchy, the need for emotional contact with others is a key part of going up the scale.

Intellectual support. Talking with others, exchanging ideas, concepts, etc. was and is important to me in my growth not only as a writer, but as a person. Networking is part of getting feedback from the world around you.

Career support. There are few occupations where interaction with other people aren't involved. Perhaps lighthouse keeper? The more I've networked, the more doors have opened up to me. Who Dares Wins Publishing came out of a conversation I had with Jen Talty about her experience with ePublishing and my desire to publish my backlist.

Networking is a two way street. You have to be open to helping others.

When I attend conferences and workshops, I've found the most important part of them are not the formal presentations and events. It is the informal networking that goes on, usually outside the formal structure. Late night discussions in the lobby; chats at meals; corresponding with those I've met after the event is over; these and more have proved very valuable.

The value of networking comes out in many ways, some very unexpected.

Tool Eight: Command

"We are all warriors in the battle of life, but some lead and others follow."
Kahlil Gibran.

You have to take charge of your career. As an author it took me a long time to accept the reality of publishing. I control the quality of the books I write. I don't control the actions of my editor, my publisher, the bookstore, etc. Trying to control those things is a waste of time and energy, and very emotionally draining. I learned to put that energy into the things I did control: my writing. To take command of that.

I also learned that I could not assume those other people were going to do their jobs well, or even at all. I thought if I didn't contact someone to check if they were doing their jobs in regard to my books, they'd appreciate not being harassed and take care of business. What I didn't realize is that there is truth to the saying the squeaky wheel gets the grease. The quiet wheel gets ignored. I always used to joke that the difference between aggressive and obnoxious is that the aggressive person has a good book while the obnoxious person has a bad one. What I was blind to, was the fact I wasn't being aggressive.

Early in my career, I expected my agent to come up with a career plan for me. It took me years before I realized that my agents could never have done this. Each of them helped me, but I had to exercise personal leadership over, my career—then ask for their help. I had to make the plan. I had to set the goals. And I had to take responsibility.

With the current flux in publishing, authors have more responsibility and opportunity than ever before. As a non-traditional publisher and author, I run a business and spend a good portion of my time doing that in addition to writing. As part of that, I have to keep current with what the latest trends and try to anticipate where publishing is going. I believe it's a very exciting time to be an author, but the ones who will succeed are the ones who are aware and take charge.

Leadership—The Problems

Most writers don't exercise personal leadership. 90% of first novels fail—often because the writer expects the agent & publisher to do things, which they don't. It sounds cynical, but expecting your publisher to promote and push your book is like expecting your OB-GYN to raise your child. Unless you are getting an advance in the six figures, the publisher is basically tossing the book out there to see if it sinks or swims.

In publishing every deal, every development, is a *good* news/*bad* news situation. Everything has two sides to it. I remember when the issue of e-books first came up years ago. It was good news because there was a new medium for books. It was bad news because things got murky with when is a book out of print?

The most recent thing I'm seeing is publishers trying to delay the e-book edition until several months after the hardcover comes out. It's a desperate measure to hold on to something that will eventually have to change. This is where you really need a good agent—to look at all angles of every deal. Every deal and event in publishing is in the gray, with both positive and negative aspects. You have to take the time to carefully analyze everything for all the angles.

The one power you have as a writer is the power to say NO.

What this means is that any deal is not necessarily a good deal. Any agent is not necessarily a good agent. Self-publishing will have it's share of successes but will have the same failure rate as trying to get traditionally published.

Leadership

A leader is a person who makes decisions and then implements a course of action. Since a successful person is someone who takes action, that person is, by definition, a leader.

The first thing a leader must do is set goals, which we discussed under Tool One. Then the leader must make a decision, leading to a course of action that implements sustained change. Ultimately, a leader must take care of himself or herself, and then those around them.

The first person you must understand how to lead is yourself. That's why I spend so much time in **AREA TWO: *WHO*,** on ***CHARACTER.*** You need to figure out your personality type and your blind spot. Successful people overcome their weaknesses, and the first step in doing that is identifying the weaknesses. This skill immediately separates those who want to be successful from the majority of the bell curve.

Special Operations Leadership

I believe the type of leadership we utilize in Special Operations is ideally suited to develop successful individual leadership in publishing. Units in Special Operations are small, and the soldiers well trained and internally motivated. Their missions are usually above the military norm. Special Forces often operates far removed from the normal military chain of command.

Whether you desire to be traditionally published and especially if you go non-traditional, no one is going to care more about your book and your career than you. In non-traditional you really can't make it on your own. You are going to have to build a team to be successful.

There are two key elements of Special Operations leadership, ***Honesty*** and ***Integrity***

Honesty

"What I want is men who will support me when I am in the wrong."

Lord Melbourne (1779–1848), British statesman. Replying to a politician who said he would support Melbourne as long as he was in the right.

Honesty is the foundation of respect. Without honesty, all other aspects of what you learn in *Write It Forward* falls apart. Special Operations Forces, which conduct covert and secret operations, actually rely on honesty a great deal. You may find that curious. But it is the very nature of their missions that requires a higher degree of internal honesty from SOF members and teams.

Honesty is your key to dealing with those around you. You cannot expect people to be honest with you, if you aren't with them. And first and foremost, you need to be honest with yourself.

Honesty is the key to developing and understanding your character. How many have gone to a therapist and lied? It's an insane situation, but a common one: people will pay large amounts of money for therapy, but withhold things about themselves for various reasons, usually embarrassment. Yet they somehow expect the therapist to be able to help them. The same is true for any of your goals and weaknesses that you tackle with *Write It Forward;* you can only help yourself, as much as you're willing to open and be honest in the exercises I've put before you.

We all have secrets, and those secrets are often rooted in our deepest fears. Bringing your secrets into the light of day seems daunting. But in reality, once you've achieved this step, the result is rarely ever as bad as you expected it to be. Most people care more about themselves than they do about you. In general, people overestimate how others are going to react to their secrets. We've discussed that as a writer, you are putting yourself out there. It's a great fear for many people but it goes with the territory.

Your honesty is the touchstone of good communication with those you interact with and those you lead. Remember, we teach people how to treat us.

I spoke with another Special Forces team leader about serving in Afghanistan. He made the point that the Afghanis treated American units differently, depending on how the American units first treated the Afghanis. Those teams that made themselves the bad-ass, but honest, sheriff in town were treated with respect. Those teams that initially negotiated from a position of weakness or tried deception were treated as weak.

As a writer if you project confidence and passion in a professional way, you will find that others in the business reflect it back. If you put yourself out there tentatively and with fear, don't expect an enthusiastic response. Everything starts with your emotions and how your project yourself out to the world.

This ties back into communication.

Integrity

The word integrity comes from the Latin word integritas, which means wholeness, completeness and entirety.

A Roman soldier, when being inspected by his Centurion, would strike his fist on the armor over his heart and shout *Integritas.* The armor was thicker there than anywhere else. In the same manner, your armor must be strongest around the most vulnerable parts of your successful character. Focusing on and building integrity is the best way to make sure that happens.

Integrity is the opposite of the emotional defenses around our defects. Integrity is the emotional defense around the part of us that is daring and willing to take risks. Remember the Terry Gilliam quote from earlier in the book. As you become more successful as an author, there will be more people criticizing what you do.

People without integrity ignore their blind spots. And they hide other aspects of their character—often from themselves—because they are afraid. Your successful goal must be completeness of **CHARACTER**.

Completeness means all parts of your **CHARACTER** are oriented toward the same goal rather than conflicting with one another. As you've learned, most people are the cause of their own failure. Accordingly, you can also be the cause of your success. In today's publishing environment, authors have more options and more opportunities than ever before.

Integrity is outward-oriented, and requires that you understand the environment in which you live, and respect and understand those with whom you interact. It requires you to make your place in the world, and to make that place count—for your own good, as well as others.

Command of self is taking action in the face of fear.

Facing and dealing with fear is at the core of your ability to move from being ordinary to successful. How you deal with fear is all about how you apply honesty and integrity in your life, your actions and your decision-making. Understanding your character and others is important. And setting goals gives you direction.

The Circle of Success tools won't change anything by themselves, though. Not until your personal command begins to break you from the chains of fear.

The Rule Of 7

There is a TV show called *Seconds from Disaster*. Each hour-long episode examines a plane crash. After watching many episodes, I started noting a pattern: A plane crash requires a minimum of 7 things to go wrong. Always, at least 1 of the 7 is human, and thus can be averted. Most of the seven are small things, but when added up, they equal catastrophe. This is why I focus on small things that disturb me, because they could be one part of the seven.

Turning this around, I also believe there is a Rule of 7 for Success. Success rarely happens in a vacuum or in a single step. While the only power you really have is to say NO, but it is often best to take every opportunity. Publishing is such a strange business, that you never know which person or opportunity will come back years later in a good or bad way.

It shocked me to hear that agents say they get about 10% of the people sending them material when requested at a conference. The other 90% don't do it. Many people feel their work isn't ready, they're afraid, etc. etc. but think of the opportunity wasted. I actually tell people to 'cheat' (rule-breaking, not a violation of integrity—there is a difference). Even if you didn't meet that agent at the conference, send them your submission anyway, saying you did meet them at the conference. They're not going to remember anyway.

The Rule of 7 for Success means that you never know what is going to happen down the line. This is why it's good to network and not burn bridges.

Catastrophe Planning

Publishing is a very fickle business. You control the writing and very little else unless you go non-traditional. So you need a backup plan. While the reason for having a Catastrophe Plan might seem obvious, there is a deeper and more positive reason to do this: it allows you to be more creative and successful.

In Special Forces, as soon as we received our mission statement and went into isolation, one of the first things we started doing was preparing our Go To Sh$% plan. This could also be called our Catastrophe Plan. It was a plan for what we would do if everything went to hell and we couldn't count on anyone else for support. Having this plan was a comfort, because it meant we were prepared.

When Arnold Schwarzenegger moved to Hollywood way back when, his Strategic Goal was to become a movie star. Think about it. Have you seen him in Pumping Iron? What a joke, right? The accent. The body. He also took night courses in Real Estate. I submit to you that he didn't take night courses because he wanted to become a realtor or ever planned to become one. He did it for the peace of mind so he could focus on pursuing his true goal.

As writers, we have to do the same thing. We can never count on our writing to support us, even if we become best-selling authors. The publishing gods are very fickle. If you are constantly stressed over making money as a writer, your writing will suffer. You need a catastrophe plan and you need it for peace of mind so you can focus on your writing and continuing to be successful.

The Advantages Of A Catastrophe Plan

- *You worst-case the scenario. You plan for the worst case so you have a 'Go To Shit' plan that helps you avoid the worst case. It relies only on you and your readily available assets*
- *If the worst case happens, you have a plan. It's better to have a plan in hand than have to make one up when bad things happen*
- *Most importantly, knowing that if things Go To Sh$% you have a plan, reduces fear and anxiety. This is key. You can put the energy you would have put into worrying into being successful*

The Future Of Publishing

There was article in the NY Times from the President of a NY Publishing company (FS&G) not long ago. He was actually complaining that descendants are re-publishing William Styron's work and not going back through the original publisher.

I find this article a signal that NY is running scared. He's claiming that the caring editorial work that Random House did needs to be a factor. Except he needs to walk his own hallways and see how much caring editorial work his editors currently do. I'm not accusing anyone of anything—nowadays the system is set up to produce books, not nurture them like it was in the good old days. An editor at a traditional publishing house is overwhelmed with the number of titles they have to deal with.

I went on an extended book tour for St. Martins, which is part of MacMillan (which Farrar, Straus & Giroux is also part of) under which Tor also falls. On the same day the SMP book came out, I had a hardcover from Tor released. I tried to get my editor and publicist at Tor to coordinate books for the tour, which their parent company was already paying for. They all work in the same building in NYC (the Flatiron building). The people at Tor could not be bothered to take the elevator a couple of flights and coordinate this, thus there were no Tor hardcovers at the book signing sites. This is more indicative of the 'caring touch' the publisher is referring to in the current publishing climate. We are always our own worst enemies and unless publishing wakes up, they will continue being their own.

Also, it's fascinating that the example the publisher uses is half-a-century old. What have you done for authors lately?

This is not a rant on my part. This is discussing reality. In Special Forces we kept the same fundamentals but we adapted to the times and technology, which is a tenet of *Write It Forward*.

During the First Gulf War, Scud missiles were a major problem if you remember. Special Operations teams were sent out to recon for those missiles without much success. After the war, 5th Special Forces Group conducted an AAR on the missile hunt. Examining what worked and what didn't work. Then they assigned a couple of very smart sergeants the task of developing a better plan to hunt Scuds on the chance we went back into Iraq. Did you hear anything about Scud missile launches during the Second Gulf War? Nada. Because the plan was damn good and it worked to perfection.

Remember, things are not changing in a linear fashion; they are changing exponentially.

eBooks are the future. That's not an emotional statement but a factual one. It doesn't matter whether I like it or not, I have to deal with it as an author and publisher. That's reality and numbers. Numbers rule in business. In essence, the most endangered species in publishing is the publisher.

The whole eBook thing has apparently touched a nerve. It's just a new medium. The essence of a book is the same.

In twenty years of writing, I've gone back and forth on things, particularly marketing. There are times I've gone all out on trying to market, only to feel like I'm in a big black hole and nothing is happening, get discouraged and quit.

About 15 years ago, when there were more independent bookstores, I sent a letter to each one of 3,500 stores in the country with about 40 signed bookplates in each letter. I received three responses. Frustrating. Yet, a couple of years ago I met someone who said he was in a small bookstore and my books were featured and the owners said they had gotten a letter from me and always remembered that. The Rule of 7.

So. You're throwing darts into a big black hole, hoping to hit something. The odds are, you won't. But if you don't throw anything, the odds are even worse.

It's frustrating.

Again. Write better books.

Publishing is the Wild West right now, with changes happening daily and most of the prognosticators from the beginning of the year already proven wrong, as they were last year.

No one. I only know the view of my own position.

Jen Talty and I formed Who Dares Wins Publishing in January 2010. At the time I was looking at it as a sideline, a way to get my *Atlantis* series back into circulation. I was busy writing my epic *Duty, Honor, Country, a Novel of West Point and the Civil War* and editing *The Jefferson Allegiance* in anticipation of sending them to my agent for sale (Jen meanwhile, slaved away full-time for the past 18 months on building the company). One could argue this was my catastrophe plan for my traditional writing career.

However, as 2011 dawned, I had to re-evaluate. 2010 was a year of drastic change. In January, eBooks constituted roughly 3% of the market. People, *experts*, said they might make it to 5 or maybe even 10% by the end of the year. They were wildly off.

I had to evaluate based not on where publishing was now, but rather where it was going to be. So I made the decision to commit to Who Dares Wins Publishing completely. Considering this is my livelihood, abandoning a proven business model for an unknown model was risky, but I've always taken chances and embraced challenges, from West Point to the Infantry to volunteering for the Green Berets and in publishing. I'm going to use my own sales numbers, not the other authors we have for the sake of privacy.

In January of 2011 I sold 347 eBooks.

In June of 2011, I sold 36,000 eBooks.

And I only sell two titles at .99; the rest of my titles range from $2.99 to $4.99, which means they earn 70% royalties on their platforms. While John Locke sold over a million books on Amazon, they were all priced at .99 except for his book on how to sell a million books on Amazon. I think what he did was quite a brilliant maneuver for his situation. My average income per eBook is roughly $1.50. My Kindle and Publt sales have increased every single week. I have twelve titles in the top 100 in their genre, and two titles in the top ten in science fiction in both the US and UK.

We just launched a brand-new automated web site thanks to Jen Talty's hard work that is already paying dividends in direct sales (which means 100% income, which beats any publisher/bookstore I know of). Our authors get 50% royalties, higher than any publisher I've heard of. (Jen and I unilaterally raised them from 40 to 50% because we felt that was fair).

I talked to a representative from Publt recently on the phone and it was enlightening. It was the first time in my 20 years as an author that a seller of books contacted me about selling more books. Radical concept. Traditional publishing has been so enraptured of the publisher-consignment outlet relationship that the author-seller-reader relationship was neglected. And the reality, talking to Barnes and Noble, is that their people at Publt get it: that it's really the author-reader relationship that sells books.

For promotion, the single most important thing is consistency. As I've noted before, this is a marathon, not a sprint.

Another key is being willing to admit when we are wrong and change. At Thrillerfest, Jen and I discussed our three-year plan. We're looking ahead and we've got some ideas to explore new markets and new technologies. Because we're a small company, we can adapt quickly.

It might be the Wild West in publishing, but as a former Green Beret, it's the kind of environment we were trained to thrive in.

This is taking **COMMAND** of my career. Regardless of your chosen publishing path, it's important you take command of your writing career. No one else is going to do it for you. You can build a team, but ultimately you have to lead yourself.

Self-Publishing

Our motto at *Write It Forward* is appropriated from the Infantry: Lead, follow or get the hell out of the way. Authors produce the books. Readers consume the books. Everyone else is in the middle, and therefore, very, very nervous. Because, in essence, the only two parts of publishing that are absolutely necessary are writers and readers. Yes, books need to be edited, marketing needs to be done, etc. etc. But much of that work can be contracted out.

It used to be publishers controlled distribution. That was their lock. If an aspiring author asked me if a publisher was legitimate or not, I told them to go to their local bookstores and ask the manager if that publisher had distribution to the store. But today, everyone has access to distribution with eBooks. And you might have a hard time in the coming years finding that bookstore manager to ask if they don't adapt.

I use to tell aspiring authors to never self-publish fiction. The reality is 99.5% of self-published fiction will fail. But given all the changes, I had to re-evaluate. The reality is 99.5% of queries to agents fail. So the odds of succeeding at self-publishing at little cost via eBooks and Print on Demand, are pretty much the same. There *are* going to be success stories coming out of the ranks of new authors among the self-published. So why not double your chances of success by continuing querying while at the same time self-publishing and self-promoting? Some will say that agents won't look at material that's been self-published. That's called an ignorant agent. The game has changed and either change with it or get the hell out of the way. BTW, the self-promoting is something traditional publishers and agents are saying authors have to do anyway. In fact, it gets to the point reading all these blogs and tweets from agents/editors, that I ask: if I, as the author, have to do all this stuff, what the heck are you doing?

The reality is that 10% of a publisher's books make 90% of their revenue. As publishers contract, the people getting cut out are the new and midlist authors. Which begs the question, where will that next 10% come from?

I argue that they will come from the self-published who do succeed. But there is an inherent flaw in that. A self-published book that
sells 5 or 6 thousand books will get interest from the Big 6 and literary
agents. Except when that author crunches the numbers, the publisher
will have to guarantee *4 times as many readers* in order to break even
with what that author is making on their own. It's a Catch-22.

All in all, I think it's an exciting time to be an author with lots of
opportunities, but only if you educate yourself and stay on top of the
latest developments and trends. This is one of the major goals of this
book and program. Authors, you must assimilate faster than publishers, bookstores, and agents are, if you want to survive. Embrace the
technology and use it to your advantage.

I was literally cursed at in social media in January of 2010 for my
predictions regarding eBooks, agents, publishers and authors. If anything, my predictions didn't go far enough.

So What Do I See Ahead?

When a major fiction author breaks from traditional publishing and
puts a book out on their own via eBook, things will drastically change.
David Morrell, who I consider a major author, already did this in 2010,
but not many noticed. Seth Godin did it in non-fiction. But when someone big-big splits, it will make traditional publishers tremble.

The 25% royalty rate for e-rights is ridiculous and has to go. 40%
is the minimum. Even then, do the math:

$9.99 eBook. Publisher gets $6.99. Author at 25% gets $1.75
$9.99 eBook. Publisher gets $6.99. Author at 40% gets $2.79
$9.99 eBook. Author goes it alone. Author gets $6.99.

So even at 40% royalty the traditional publisher has to sell 2.5
times as many copies as the author doing it alone. And what exactly
does the publisher do for that money now? Not distribution. Placement, if they pay. Copyediting, which can be outsourced by the independent author. A *stamp* of approval. But if it's a brand name author,
that doesn't matter. No one goes into a bookstore and says, "gimme
a Random House". They do go in and say "gimme a Nora Roberts."

Many agencies are going to try to straddle a very difficult line of selling to traditional publishing while also bringing books out on their own, particularly their authors' backlist and promising books they can't place with a traditional house but they see value in. The conflict of interest will put them in a tough spot. It's going to be a black or white situation. Either become your own publishing house or stay traditional. I actually predict that there will be some mergers between publishers and agents, where the line between the two will blur. The reality is that agents are 90% of the gatekeeping of quality control in publishing. Publisher held the lock on distribution. Their lock is over. Once the 50% tipping point is reached *(and my #1 prediction is it will be reached in 2011)* where more eBooks are bought than print books, the whole ball game is going to change. B&N.com has just announced they sell more eBooks than print books.

Enhanced eBooks will begin to multiply. Just in this book we have added hyperlinks to various blogs, books and websites to make it easy for the reader to check out the various things we are discussing. You will also see embedded video and music, although the reality is only the iPad really supports this now. One thing I do believe will be constant is that mixing media doesn't work well. This is why film trailers for books are pretty much a waste of money for 99.5% of authors who do them, unless you can do something like Jane Austen's Fight club. Still, hits to a YouTube video clip does not equate to the same number in sales, but it does create a bit of buzz. My YouTube clip on Special Forces is closing in on 100,000 views but I really haven't seen any crossover.

Another possibility are alternate versions of books and additional material, including *author cuts*. Much like you can get the director's cut of a DVD, authors will be able to include material that would have ended up on the floor of their editor's office. Also, they could give two or more different endings to a book. They can also add in comments about the writing of the book, much like Baldacci has already done.

More *shorts* on specific non-fiction topics. This is a focus at Who Dares Wins Publishing. Priced at $2.99 (less than a cup of coffee at

Starbucks) and at least 10,000 words long, these will be non-fiction works that address something the reader specifically wants answered. For example, we just released *The Writer's Conference Guide: How to Get the Most out of Your Time and Money.* This book describes how to find, prepare for, spend your time at, and reap the benefits after a conference. For someone who is going to plunk down a $400 registration fee plus travel, plus hotel, and most importantly time, for a writer's conference, it really makes sense to spend $2.99 for advice on how to make the most of it all.

2010 was an unstable year. Publishing began reacting to changes, when they should have been acting in years prior (a tenet of *Write It Forward*). We saw publishers create vanity presses. We saw agents become publishers. Authors started skipping publishers all together. We saw a publisher in mass market go direct to digital. We've seen agents close doors. We hear smaller advances, higher sell-through rate, and more authors being dropped. We saw Amazon cut a major publisher out of the picture. In a nutshell, publishing is being forced to changed and while they fight the publishing Borg, many of us are embracing it. We're acting and taking control of our careers. We are assimilating to the future because the future is here.

2010 brought the digital book and eReaders to an equal playing field, whether NY wants to face it or not. You can't get on an airplane in today's world and not see some sort of reading device and it's not just the younger generation using these devices. We're all using them. The Nook, The Kindle and The iPad are here to stay. Add Wi-Fi and 3G capabilities and the reduced pricing 2010 has also brought, there isn't any reason not to embrace the technology, as we did with computers, laptops and cell phones.

The future is going to continue on this road. There are more forks now than ever before, each leading to a new and exciting, though sometimes scary opportunity. It is the year of the Author which is why we *Write It Forward*. For too long writers have focused on getting an agent, a book contract, etc. etc. but ultimately, what you really want are readers to buy your books, not agents and publishers. It's a new paradigm that few are taking the lead in. 2011 and beyond is going to be great for writers willing to look to the future.

Can Any Writer Self-Publish?

The answer is a big fat **YES**. Technology has made this a relatively simple process. I say relatively because there is a steep learning curve and even after you've *learned* the basics, if you want to do it right and maximize your efforts in order to increase your sales, you're going to have to make this your full time job. It's not a get rich quick scheme, but you can turn a pretty profit.

When I made the leap into indie publishing I created a team. The foundation of that team is myself and my business partner Jen Talty. While my backlist is what launched this company (and I would have self-published it regardless) the success is because Jen and I work together in making sure we are making the most of our options.

And there are a lot of options out there for the author who wants to self-publish. You can use a vanity press, though if you are going to invest in your future as a writer there are other ways to self-publish. You can go with something like Smashwords, which is a distributor and let them be your publisher and distributor to various ebookstores. LuLu is another option for both eBooks and POD. You can just publish on Kindle. Or B&N. Both stores have made the process pretty painless.

Which brings me to the element of time. Yes, anyone can self-publish. But in order to be successful, you have to invest a huge amount of time and energy into finding what will be the best option for you. It is not one-size fits all. What works for one, might not work for another. And, all I've discussed so far is getting your book ready for publication. And just the book. Not the cover, etc. But the bottom line is, anyone who puts their mind to it, can self-publish their book.

The question you need to ask yourself is does the option of self-publishing fit into my strategic overall plan as a writer? It always comes back to your individual goals.

Should Anyone Self-Publish Their Book?

The answer to this question is a big fat **DEPENDS**. Why? When we first started with Who Dares Wins Publishing, we believed the most successful self-published authors came from two backgrounds. The first being previously published authors with backlist. We found this to be true as the *Atlantis* and *Area 51* series are our number one selling eBook on all platforms.

The second background would be a non-fiction author with a platform. We found this to be true with six of our authors. Myself, along with Amy Shojai, Victoria Martinez, Natalie C. Markey, Kristen Lamb, and Joy E. Held have strong platforms with quality non-fiction books that sell well.

However, we used to believe that if you don't fit into those two categories you might as well pack up and go home. That isn't necessarily the case anymore. The key is content. Do you have quality content? Is your material, whether it be fiction or non-fiction well written, edited and is it something readers want? The other key is promotion. If you plan on simply putting your stuff out there and think the readers are just going to flock to you, well good luck with that. You have to be willing to promote, and promote hard.

It's a wonderful time to be an author because the author has a lot more control if he or she wants it and with that control comes a greater chance of success.

Tips For Unpublished Authors Who Want To Self-Publish

This section is all about taking ***command*** of your career. With that comes responsibility. We've spent a lot of time talking about our goals and how we plan on achieving our goals. I didn't jump into self-publishing without a plan. Before the first *Atlantis* book was even released, Jen Talty and I wrote out our first business plan. That plan has changed drastically over the last couple of years because as we changed and adapted to the publishing industry so did our business plan.

I've done several conferences this year and noticed a distinct change in the air regarding publishing. Agents and editors seem more subdued, no longer swaggering around as if they held the keys to the kingdom. Because they don't. Traditional publishing held the keys in terms of distributions for many decades. They no longer do. I am currently selling more copies of my *Area 51* series in a day than Random House did in six months. I have two titles in the top 10 on Amazon science fiction and one in top ten in men's adventure.

At these conferences, I'm asked by writers, whether they should self-publish rather than seek traditional publishing. I've thought a long time about this, putting myself in that position, but using my 20 years of experience in traditional publishing and 2 years in indie publishing and having been successful in both.

My answer: No. I wouldn't self-publish my first manuscript. I'd be querying the traditional publishing route (primarily agents) while focusing on writing my second manuscript. Then when I finished that, would I self-publish if I hadn't gotten an agent?

No. I'd still keep querying, getting feedback from beta readers, and be writing my third manuscript. Also, I'd have the three books be part of a series in terms of theme and content. Same characters, setting, whatever, but they should essentially be the same genre. When I finished that third book would I self-publish?

Yes. If I had gotten positive feedback from beta readers and perhaps an agent or editor and did the work to make the book better, I'd put all three titles up. Then spend 50% of my time promoting while writing my fourth book.

The problem right now is too many writers are putting their first manuscript up and spending 75% of their time trying to promote as they try to write their second book. The focus isn't on the writing, it's on the selling. And sales are going to be terrible. I'm selling 2,500 eBooks a day and honestly, most new writers, with no backlist, would be very happy to sell that in a year (ask my business partner her numbers with an ePublisher for a year and she'd tell you the same thing). I didn't sell my first manuscript. I was on manuscript #3 before I got an agent and rewrote the book based on his comments, and then sold it. And now, as I go through my early books as we upload them, I cringe sometimes at the writing (they're great books, buy them, yes, right now), but I've learned so much over the 20 years I've been writing full time. I've learned more in the past two years than the first 18. I can see where I had point of view problems. Sentence structure problems. Character development.

The more I think about it, the more I feel for a new writer with no backlist, the most important thing to do is write three quality manuscripts first, before investing heavily in promotion. The investment is time. That is our most valuable resource. It needs to be spent on learning the craft of writing.

Please understand I'm not saying don't self-publish. What I'm actually suggesting is to wait before you have more than one quality book before really jumping into the self-publishing camp.

There is no right or wrong publishing path anymore. One of the best things I heard came from Steve Feldberg of Audible.com at Thrillerfest when said that he didn't think there were any alternative forms of publishing left—that its all publishing. I believe that is true, whether you self publish or are traditionally published you are a REAL author.

Using *Write It Forward* there is more we can do. Remember the plan? Look several books ahead. Have some commonality in a series of books. Make the first book kick-ass and let the agent know that you have a long term plan.

What the internet has done is interesting. Rather than broaden things, it's made things more specialized and niche. This is both good and bad. It means you can focus on specific markets. But it also means people aren't getting the breadth and depth of information they used to. I've found in my current WIP that I am going back to using books as reference material rather than the internet. The books give me depth, more details I wouldn't have found on the internet, and more narrative.

I taught at the Northwest Institute of Literary Arts MFA program. One thing quite a few of the attendees asked about was how to get gigs teaching writing. After all, to be honest, often the goal of an MFA student is to become an MFA teacher, not necessarily become a published author or make a living writing. Even for people who don't have MFAs though, I recommend doing some teaching.

Tool Nine: Complete

You have to design your circle of success using all your answers through the nine Special Forces to support your strategic goal. Then you must periodically re-assess and change when needed. Write out a complete plan of action for completing your strategic goal, using all the eight previous tools.

This is a spiral of success, not a linear path. It's an upward spiral, where you revisit each Tool, but with more knowledge and experience, so that you can constantly improve.

Execution

Mission Execution—The Problems

We can have a great, well thought out plan, but even if all the elements are in place, but we do not synchronize them and act on them we may not succeed. As writers, our biggest asset is our time. If we do not use that effectively and efficiently, we will have problems in the execution of our plan. It is important to look closely at our strategic goals and if all supporting goals are aligned. We need to consider our environment and how that affects how we work. And we need to take control of our career. All of these things must be synchronized in order to achieve success.

Mission Execution—The Solutions
- *Isolation is used to prepare for the mission*
- *A Briefback is conducted to coordinate the mission*

- *An After Action Review is used to evaluate and adapt*
- *Rule breaking is needed to succeed*

Isolation

As a writer, isolation is you taking the time you need to hone your craft and constantly improve your writing. Remember **content** is **king**. Without a quality product, your promotional efforts will eventually fall to the wayside.

A form of isolation at the most base level that I believe is essential for a writer is to turn off the Internet while creating. I turn off my wireless and set a timer when I'm focused on writing. It allows me to focus on what I'm doing. The Internet simply provides too many distractions.

Briefback

At the end of isolation, just prior to departing on the mission, an A-Team has to give a Briefback. This is done in the secure facility. The commander of the Forward Operating Base that is deploying the team is there. Along with his staff. And coordinating personnel involved in the mission such as Air Force liaison, etc.

The goal of the Briefback are several.
- *To show we have a good plan*
- *To show the entire team knows the plan*
- *To make sure all support personnel are on the same sheet of music*
- *To get the commander's approval for the mission (I have seen plans get rejected and the team have to start over)*

As a writer, I think you should *briefback* your book with someone. Talk your book out as much as you can. Discuss the characters, the plot, the conflict, the point of view, etc. etc. Have the people you give the briefback to ask you questions. In my Writing Workshop, we spend the entire morning writing 1 sentence—that original idea. Using the synergy of the group, we often come up with some really good material. I discussed using a group like

Susan Mallery's earlier. I don't think any writer can succeed without creative help.

As a publishing company, Jen Talty and I constantly briefback our business plan. We spent a week at Thrillerfest and when we weren't networking or giving workshops we were looking at our business plan and making adjustments so we can take this to the next level.

Networking and finding other writers with similar goals as yours can be very beneficial and allow you a forum in which to do a writer's briefback to get feedback.

After Action Reviews

Once you've implemented your plan, it's time to use another Special Forces tool—the After Action Review (AAR). This is used by Special Forces to objectively determine if a mission's goal has been achieved. In fact, whenever you think you've finished doing something significant, you should conduct an AAR.

A person that won't look closely at themselves is someone who is doomed to keep doing the same things wrong again and again.

Because simulated combat exercises are so difficult to observe and judge, the military designed the AAR to help the participants figure out what happened. It was only in the late '90s that the business world began picking up the concept, most likely a result of Army officers filtering into the civilian world and bringing what they had learned with them. A Harvard Business School professor wrote an article about it in the Harvard Business Review in 1993, which I suppose made it more highbrow than a squad of grunts sitting around trying to figure out what just happened. The most critical aspect of having an effective AAR is honesty. The first, and most important, question to be answered is, *was the goal or mission accomplished?* Given that your goal or mission was originally stated clearly in one sentence, the answer should be clear.

I have read several business books where it is said an AAR should not judge success or failure. I disagree with that. Why not? The theory is that focusing on success or failure will cause emotional conflict—if that's the case, then so be it. We succeed. We fail. We learn, adjust and move on. Successful people have to break through the conflict that comes with not succeeding all the time.

Remember the stages of change: denial, anger, bargaining, depression, acceptance. If failure at a goal is a conflict for you, it's one of your blind spots. Work through these changes until you've conquered the associated fear.

If the answer is yes, you achieved your goal, then pat yourself on the back, then see what fine-tuning needs to be done. If the answer is no, hunker down until the smoke clears—until you have solid answers from your AAR and know what changes need to be made to your plan.

With both my writing career and Who Dares Wins Publishing, I periodically conduct After Action Reviews. I always find better and more efficient ways to accomplish my goals.

Steps for an effective AAR.

- *Did you achieve your goal*
- *Review your plan. Did you follow your plan? If not, note the exceptions and variations you made*
- *Review the preparation for the activity—which means once more go through all the Forces listed in this book, and now that the plan has been executed, determine if each Tool was effectively applied to your plan*
- *Summarize the events as they occurred, using a detailed timeline, with no commentary. Just the facts. Build a complete timeline of action*
- *Focus on why each specific action was taken. Whether each step of the plan was followed, or deviated from (which is not necessarily a bad thing)*
- *Give particular focus to when fear played a role in your actions—this is the most difficult part of the AAR, but the most critical—fear is most likely where your actions diverged from your plan*

- *Summarize areas of plan improvement and refinement, as well as alternative actions you could have taken to achieve a more successful result*

Rule Breaking

To be successful, you are going to have to break some rules. If you do the same as everyone else, you're the same as everyone else. In Special Forces our unofficial motto was: *If you ain't cheating, you ain't trying.*

But beware you don't break the three rules of Rule Breaking:

The paradoxical rules of rule breaking.

1. *Know the rule (breaking a rule because you don't know or understand it, is just being dumb)*
2. *Have a good reason for breaking the rule (I ask WHY a lot in my workshops. I don't believe there are any rules of writing— you just need a good reason why you are doing something)*
3. *Accept the consequences of breaking the rule (if it worked, you're a genius. If it didn't, figure out what went wrong, reboot and restart)*

A Career Plan

A while ago I asked Susan Wiggs for some career advice. We'd taught together for seven straight years at the Maui Writers Retreat and Conference. She also lives one island south of me. I noticed the other day while driving through the rain, and then when I looked south, the sun was shining on her island for some reason. A conspiracy perhaps.

Anyway, she emailed me back within 20 minutes of my query with a very detailed explanation of the route she followed for success.

First, Susan said she studied successful authors in her genre. This is the author dissection we discussed earlier. She looked for the patterns.

Second, what she came up with was a plan to write three books. Since they were romances, she couldn't use the same protagonist in every book; so she looked at a unifying concept. She decided on a fictional town. Suzanne Brockman uses a Navy SEAL team. This gives reader continuity. I'm using West Point as my unifying concept in my current series.

Third, you need a unifying theme. In romance, well, it's usually some form of romance. I'm using the theme of loyalty versus honor. I'm applying that theme on two levels: personal for the characters; and also in the big picture because my focus is on the Civil War.

Fourth, the goal is then to sell the heck out of the first book and get a commitment from the publisher to push the numbers on the three books. Now that is out of your control. Both Susan and I have experienced publishers that didn't push a series.

I think though, if you approach agents and publishers with a plan, you have a much better success of the plan working than not having a plan.

In fact, I was on an agent panel at Pacific Northwest Writers (no idea why I was on panel—guess because my agent was sitting next to me). And I mentioned the idea of having a plan. After the panel was over, one of the agents told me in all the years he'd been agenting, no one had ever approached him with a plan. He said he'd love it if writers had one.

I think that is the Catch-22 that a lot of agents and editors can't get past, they would love a new author to have a plan, but they don't have the time or energy to teach you how to develop one. So we're still working on the *throw 100 new books against the wall and hope 1 sticks* paradigm. I really think we need to get smarter.

The Circle Of Success

WHAT: Set and align goals.
WHY: State your intent.
WHERE: Conduct an Area Study.
CHARACTER: Understand self & others.
CHANGE: Change using the three steps.
COURAGE: Understand fear and the blind spot.
COMMUNICATE: Use effective communication.
COMMAND: Use personal and team leadership.
COMPLETE: Put it all together for mission execution.

Write It Forward works circular. A successful author will continually assess and reassess their goals and plan of action in order to continue their path of success.

In conclusion, YOU are in command of your career. It's time to *Write It Forward* and dare to succeed.

Appendix

Getting Your Novel Published Traditionally

You've finished your manuscript and now it's burning a hole through your desktop. You desperately want to start making submissions.

STOP.

I recommend you do two things *before* you start marketing a manuscript.

1. Start writing your next one. You learned so much writing the first, that your second is bound to be better. Most authors do not get published on their first try out the gate. Don't pin all your hopes on the first one and the best way to do that is to start writing the second. This also prevents you from spending an entire year trying to market the first and ending up with just a pile of rejection slips. At least at the end of the year, at the very least, you can have a pile of rejection slips *and* another manuscript ready to market. I was on manuscript #3 with hundreds of rejections on file before I got my first book deal. And I know for a fact that I wouldn't have gotten that book deal if I had not had three manuscripts in hand.

2. Let the manuscript sit for at least two weeks before making submissions. As you read the following pages, the one adjective I use over and over again with regards to the publishing world is *SLOW*. No one else is in any rush so you have to fight spinning your wheels. You're only going to get one shot at

each agent and publishing house you send your submission to; it is best to make sure it is your best one. Let the manuscript sit for a couple of weeks, then pick it up and read it very critically. Rewrite. Edit. Clean it up.

If you've done those two things, then you are ready to start thinking about marketing your book. I recommend you take the book process and work it backward to get to your starting point in trying to sell it. Think of the ultimate buyer, the person standing in the store. How do they choose a book? Don't you think editors and agents think about that quite a bit?

The critical components that editors and agents (and readers) are looking for in a novel are good characters revolving around a great idea.

Not only does the idea by itself have to be top-notch, but it also has to fit the publisher's needs at the time.

The key to selling your novel is to communicate to the agent/editor the excitement you feel about your book. You started writing an entire novel based on your original idea because it excited you—try to get that excitement across to the editor and agent as best you can. Don't let format stymie you in that attempt. Everyone can follow a formula. The key is to get someone emotionally involved in the story you wrote.

I don't think you should "write for the market" but you most definitely need to understand the market when attempting to break into it. Your original idea is the first thing that gets looked at, long before your writing does. Your background—and I mean more than just your writing background—also plays a determining role in how a publisher looks at a submission.

A common lament among writers is, *"If I could only get my manuscript read. I know a publisher would buy it."* There is a flaw in the logic of that statement that most people never consider. As I mentioned earlier, how many of you go to a bookstore, completely read a book, and *then* buy it? To expect agents and editors to do what you don't do is not fair. Also, it makes no sense. Most people buy a book from an unknown author based on reading the cover copy (your cover letter and partial synopsis) and maybe looking at the first couple of pages. In other words they buy it the same way an agent is going to take you on, or a publisher will offer you a contract.

To expect someone to invest the time into reading something of questionable value to them is naive in this business. A person in the store is going to put down her hard-earned money to buy a book. To an agent or editor, time is money. For them to invest the time to read your manuscript, they have to expect a reasonable return on that investment. And remember, *every* writer thinks his manuscript gives a great return.

Note: You should not start marketing a manuscript until it is done. I have seen new writers—with only a partial manuscript and an outline—try to approach agents and publishers at conferences. Their feeling seems to be that they will do the work to finish the rest of the manuscript if they find someone interested in it. I'm sorry to say, but that really doesn't fly in the face of the realities of the business. As I noted earlier, in the majority of cases, writers have several completed manuscripts before they get published. This is true for fiction, but not necessarily for non-fiction.

There Is No Secret Handshake

I say this because I see very strong emotions at writers' conferences. A constant asking of the same questions (most of which are answered in this book), with the feeling seeming to be that suddenly some author or, most especially, some editor or agent will suddenly leap to their feet and give the "secret" to getting published.

Another thing I see at conferences are writers getting confused by the different perspectives that are offered. I watch writers listen to authors all week long, then when the editors and agents show up on the weekend, all the same questions get asked and the answers from those on the buying end are attended to more carefully than those on the selling end, yet writers are going to be on the selling end. I can tell you how to sell a manuscript—an editor can tell you how he or she buys a manuscript. The two are not necessarily equivalent unless you want that specific editor to buy your manuscript. That editor represents his or her own views and the buying policies of that particular publisher. My perspective is being an author in the world of publishing, which has a variety of places to sell your work to.

At this point your manuscript is done and ready to market. As you read the following sections, try to follow the methodology I used. First you must find the right target. Then you must do a submission, which may well be the most important piece of work you do as an author.

The Submission

The first step in the long road to getting traditionally published.

The submission is the first step in entering the world of traditional publishing and, for most writers, the last. (Note for the purposes of this section consider the terms submission and query mean the same thing—also, this is the same thing you will send to agents). Understanding the flow of the submission will greatly increase your chances of receiving a good look. The process I describe below will make more sense if you think of it as a replication of the flow a person goes through entering a bookstore and perusing a book for purchase.

Step One: Find The Right Place To Send It

The initial thing you must determine is who to send your submission to, in the same manner that the book buyer walks to the part of the bookstore that has the type of books she enjoys reading.

Whenever I look at a book on the shelf, my eye automatically goes to the imprint on the spine that says who the publisher is. Sometimes, though, be aware that the name listed may be an imprint of a larger house. To find the publishing house, turn to the copyright page, which will usually have the publisher's address, listed. Imprints are the way a large house breaks down inside of itself to have various smaller parts.

There are numerous publications such as *The Novel And Short Story Writer's Market* that list publishers and their needs and requirements. These books give both the address and what each one wants in the way of a submission. The information listed also tells you what type of books they specialize in.

When preparing to market a manuscript, my agent always says you have to "know the scorecard." Know who is who. You have to do the same.

Understand also that the corporate take-overs and buy-outs have changed the face of publishing. Bantam, Doubleday, Dell was bought by Random House. Houses are eating each other up ferociously and you should know who is who because different imprints in the same house won't compete against themselves for the same manuscript. Ultimately this is one of many reasons why you need an agent, but let's hold off on that until I talk about agents.

Step Two: Prepare Your Submission

When you find a publisher listed address it by name to the appropriate editor. Although some publishers will look at unsolicited manuscripts, the majority of entries in the MARKET read like this:

"HOW TO CONTACT: Query with outline/synopsis and 2 sample chapters with SASE. Simultaneous submissions OK. Reports in 6 to 8 weeks."

Each one might be slightly different but if you send each the same thing you'll get looked at and it will save you quite a bit of time. Ninety-nine percent of agents and editors will accept the general format I give here. Even if a publishing house says it will look at unsolicited manuscripts, I recommend never sending one out unless it's preceded by a query and the manuscript is requested.

You can take the time to match your submission to the exact specifications in the Writer's Market, but that can be time-consuming. Also, there is a trend now where some agents and publishers just want a query letter or email submission, and then they'll request the synopsis and sample chapters if interested, and then they'll request the manuscript if still interested. I wouldn't do this as it adds an extra step to the process and every extra step increases the chance of rejections. I highly recommend sending everyone the same thing: A cover letter; a synopsis; sample chapters; and a SASE. However, for an e-submission you are often forced to conform to their requirements.

Before I go into the details of each, let me give you some general guidelines—and yes, I know you will tell me you have heard different from Agent So and So and Editor What's Her Name at that big New York publisher, but what I'm giving you here are the general rules; ignore it at your own risk.

1. All correspondence should be typed. Handwritten material does not fly.

2. Make sure the typing is clear. Use a new ribbon, laser cartridge, whatever. Hard as it is to believe, agents and editors do get material so faded or poorly printed it is difficult to read. Difficult to read equals a no-go.

3. Use white, 20 lb. paper. Do not use erasable bond paper. Your cover letter can be on higher quality paper. Do not use colored paper to try and get attention. You don't want the attention it will bring forth.

4. Use a plain type style. Don't try using weird fonts or graphics. In this day of a million fonts available in your computer, keep it simple. A Courier 12, Geneva 12, etc. work fine. Use a decent sized font, particularly in your manuscript. I often get manuscript pages on which the font is so small it gets difficult to read. Use a font that averages out to about 250 words per full manuscript page, give or take 5%.

5. There should be no visible corrections on your cover letter.

6. Have one-inch margins all around.

7. The manuscript is double-spaced (you might be able to get away with single or space and a half on your synopsis to get it down to one page).

8. All material, to include sample chapters or the manuscript, should be unbound.

9. Your name or title should be on every piece of paper.
10. Anything longer than one page should be numbered.

A Cover Letter Or Query

The first line of your query letter must grab the reader because it is the first (and maybe the last) thing the person opening your package will read. It is the same as the inside flap of the book in the bookstore that our book buyer is looking at.

What is the hook for your manuscript? Why will they want to buy it? No matter how good your manuscript is, if you don't write a good cover letter, it will never get read. My suggestion is that you use your story's original idea as your opening line: "What if . . ." Doing that serves two purposes: it gets the reader's attention, and it plants that original idea in the reader's head as she looks through the rest of the submission.

I suggest *not* starting out with the following lines:

- *Enclosed you will find . . .* Everyone is sending essentially the same thing. The editor/agent expects to find what is enclosed—a submission. This opening doesn't grab anything when it is seen fifty times a day.
- *I've just written my first novel and I'd like you to take a look at it . . .*
- *I just know you will love this . . .*

Go to the bookstore and look at book jackets. Note how they put *NY Times Best-selling Author* etc. on the cover. Well, since you aren't a NY Times Bestseller, look for the ones that have some sort of catchy phrase on the top back. For example on a book I have here, *A nuclear holocaust is just a button away . . . and someone's about to push it*. This would be a good opening line for your cover letter; except for the fact this storyline has been beaten to death.

Below, in the section on the synopsis, I talk about overusing adjectives and praising your own work. That applies here too. Let the facts speak for themselves.

After a paragraph or two on the novel, grabbing the editor's attention and making her drool with anticipation to look at your synopsis, then move on. Include not only a sales pitch for the manuscript to the publisher but also a sales pitch for yourself. The manuscript is an extension of you. What special background do you have that would make her want to see what you have done? This means not only any writing background you have, but also your background as far as the story goes. My years in the Special Forces certainly made some editors take a longer look at my query letter concerning a book about Special Forces. These paragraphs are your writing resume. If they accept your book they are hiring you. This is the equivalent of the author blurb on the inside back cover of a book. Often people buy books because the author has an interesting background; don't you think editors do the same?

This does not mean you won't get looked at it if your background doesn't have much direct application to your subject matter and you have little writing experience, but editors and agents also remember what Mark Twain said, *"Write what you know."* If your job or background in any way applies to what you've written, make sure you mention that.

As far as the paradox many lament of putting writing credentials in the cover letter, yet they haven't been published, unless you've been published in something noteworthy that you've been paid for, don't clutter up the letter with such information. Editors and agents understand you're a new author trying to break through.

Above I said make a sales pitch to the publisher, but I recommend not marketing the book. What's the difference? The sales pitch to the publisher consists of telling them what the great idea you have is. Marketing is telling the publisher who you think will want to read your novel. I've talked to agents and editors about this and for fiction they pretty much agree that you shouldn't do that for several reasons. One is that they consider themselves the expert on the market. Another is that you will probably be wrong in your estimates. Let the work speak for itself.

Be very, very careful if you try to be humorous. In a contest of submissions I just judged the one cover letter where the writer tried to be humorous was the absolute worst turn-off. I felt as if the writer were treating me like an idiot. Most of us aren't that funny. I advise staying away from trying to be funny. Unless of course you've written a humorous book in which case your cover letter better have the agent or editor rolling on the floor. As an aside here, think about what I wrote earlier about dialogue in a novel. Now think of the difference between someone like Dave Barry being funny using just the written word and a standup comic. Written humor is extremely difficult to pull off.

Your cover letter must be one page. No more than that. Sad to say it's a volume business. An agent I knew said he knows within twenty seconds if a submission is worth looking at any further. From my own experience a reader can tell very quickly whether something is worth looking further at.

Address it to the editor or agent listed in personally. Don't worry about who is really going to look at it. It's better than addressing it to "Hey you." In fact, give the publisher a call and ask whoever answers the phone if that editor still works there. Editors tend to move around quite a bit. The initial editors I started with at three different houses are no longer there.

End the cover letter with a polite thanks to the editor/agent for his/her time. Naturally, the cover letter should be an example of your best writing. Misspelling or poor grammar and you're not even out of the starting block.

You can also add a last sentence giving some factual information about the manuscript such as: *This is an 85,000 word science fiction manuscript.*

When you think cover letter, think book jacket for a hard cover book.

If they like your cover letter it means they like your idea. The major purpose of the cover letter is to get the reader to want to read your synopsis. That's it. Simply to get them to turn the page and look at your synopsis.

I just talked to an agent who told me he could pretty much tell whether he could sell a manuscript based completely on reading the cover letter! Just like the person in the bookstore who makes a decision to buy or not buy your book based simply on the cover jacket copy.

Bob Mayer
PO Box 3604
Boulder, CO 80307
(303) XXX-XXXX

29 April 2000
Presidio Press
31 Pamaron Way
Novato, CA 94949

Dear Ms. ——,

What if a secret organization of West Point Graduates has been covertly manipulating our government's policies for the past fifty years and now appears to be planning a coup against the President?

THE LINE is the story of Boomer Watson, an officer in the Army's elite Delta Force and Major Benita Trace, assigned to a headquarters in Hawaii where the President will be arriving in one week to give a speech at the 56th anniversary of the attack on Pearl Harbor. Each stumbles across clues pointing to both the existence of The Line and the apparent coup—when they get together they realize it is up to them to stop the impending assassination.

But all is not as it appears—from an apparently botched covert mission into the Ukraine to stop nuclear terrorism; to underwater fights to the death in the waters off Hawaii; to murder on the sidelines of the Army-Navy game in Philadelphia; to the movement of shadowy military forces to Oahu; to the recovery of a secret diary buried in Custer's grave at West Point—it soon becomes clear that more is going on than even Boomer and Trace suspect and the novel builds to a shattering climax on the morning of December 7th as the President prepares to make his speech over the watery grave of the Arizona .

I have eight novels accepted for publication, three of which have been published. As specific background for this novel I graduated from West Point in 1981 and served in the Green Berets as A-Team Leader and Battalion Operations Officer for ten years.

This is a 100,000 word thriller. I appreciate your taking the time to review this submission and look forward to hearing from you.
Sincerely,

The Outline/Synopsis

Again, one page. You will hear other opinions, some ranging up to ten or twenty pages. I say one page simply because I take the editors' and agents' perspective. I don't think you are going to hook them with five pages of synopsis if they don't read past page one. And you may turn them off on page three if they do. Contrary to what you instinctively think, I have found that the more someone puts down the more chance they turn the reader *off* rather than hook the reader. Remember they were hooked by your cover letter. A long synopsis might make them wiggle off the hook because there's a good chance you'll put something they won't like the more you write. I really, really, recommend no more than two pages in a synopsis, and truly think it should be one page.

I just read a four page synopsis someone sent me to review and I asked a ton of questions because the more he put in the synopsis the more questions were raised. If he had been more succinct, I would have had fewer questions.

"Oh my Gosh," you say. "How am I going to get four hundred pages of manuscript down to one page?"

It isn't easy. This can take weeks to do, but do it you must. Look at the book jackets for similar books to what you've written. Guess what? They were written in collaboration between published writers and publishers. So be sneaky. Write a book jacket for your book except you are also telling the entire story. A book jacket, when spread out on an eight and half by eleven piece of paper is only two or three paragraphs, so you actually have more room than the poor editor does when she tries to prepare copy for a jacket.

In your manuscript you will have so many important things (*everything's* important you cry) that it is bewildering to condense. Something you can try is letting someone who has read the book summarize it and see what he comes up with. His distance from the writing might allow him to do it more easily.

The best synopses of my books that I have read were my reviews in Publishers Weekly. In those, the reviewer gets the story down to one paragraph. I suggest perusing PW and seeing how a book similar to your own was summarized. Another method is to go to your local bookstore and get some old publishers' catalogues and see how they pitched their books. Don't you think it would be very worthwhile to pitch your book to that publishing house in the same manner?

Although many people feel this one page synopsis to be very unfair, if you look at it from a business perspective, it really isn't. What does a reader do in a bookstore? Look at a book cover, then the jacket or back page to read the less-than-one-page partial synopsis on the jacket. If that doesn't interest them, they don't even bother to flip it open. Neither will an editor or agent.

Common Mistakes To A Synopsis

Too Long
I beat people to death with the one page rule. Can you go longer? Yes. But every page you go over, realize that you exponentially increase the odds of losing the interest of the reader.

Too Much Detail In Certain Areas And Not Enough In Others
You always have some great ideas and plot twists that you want to mention. Forget about them. The synopsis is an *overview.*

Making The Synopsis A List Of Bullets
First this happens. Then that. Then this. Then that. Did you ever see a book jacket that looked like that? The synopsis should be prose.

Too Many Adjectives
This is an intriguing and fascinating story about a fierce, dedicated, Viking warrior who plunders his rapacious way across

Europe told in a scintillating manner, great blah, fantastic blah, blah, blah.

I can just see an editor responding, "Yes, normally we publish non-intriguing, boring books, but since yours is intriguing and fascinating—because *you* say so in your synopsis—we most certainly want it."

Just as you have to cut the fat in your book, you have to get rid of the fat in your synopsis. Editors expect good manuscripts to be intriguing, exciting, captivating, etc. etc. You, as the author, using those adjectives to describe your own work, is a waste of space. Use verbs as your power words—not adjectives and adverbs. This also goes for your cover letter. Let the work speak for itself.

The "I Don't Know What The Story Is About?" Syndrome

There are few things worse than finishing someone's synopsis and still not having a clue what the manuscript is about. Give it to a stranger you meet on the street—or better yet in the bookstore—and see if they understand it. Have them tell you what they think your story is about after reading your synopsis. You might be surprised at the feedback.

The "You Have Eight Great Stories Here In Your Synopsis But What's The Book About?" Syndrome

Too often synopsis turns out to be a muddle of subplots that leaves the reader wondering what the main story is about. Wondering what—you got it—the original idea is.

The "I Don't Know What Kind Of Story This Is? What's The Market?" Syndrome

I've read synopsis and then scratched my head wondering if this was a science fiction book? A fantasy? A children's book? Just where the heck in the bookstore are we supposed to stack this sucker anyway? You are supposed to cover this in—you got it—the cover letter (pun intended) but if it's not clear in the synopsis, it makes the editor/

agent wonder if it will be clear when they read the manuscript. If they read it.

What's The Story? Who Are The Characters?

The "These characters sound very good but what's the story?" versus "This story sounds great but are there any characters in it?" Both are extremes and both are wrong.

The "Gee, It Sure Would Have Been Nice To Know Your Surprise Ending, But I Don't Have The Time To Respond To Your Query Because You Left Me Hanging," Syndrome

Tell the ending. The editor doesn't want to play guessing games and too often people promise much more than they actually deliver in surprise endings.

There is another angle to take sometimes with synopsis, particularly if your manuscript does not fit into a specific genre, is more character oriented, or perhaps is humorous. I think about some books that if you wrote a synopsis on them, first off, there would not be much of a story and secondly there would be no hint as to the real uniqueness of the writing. For example, Anne Tyler's *Breathing Lessons* would make a most boring synopsis.

I mention this because I think it is important not to sacrifice the uniqueness of your book to try and fit a "format." The page you use for a synopsis might be better used in some cases to give examples of some highlights of the writing. If your book is a series of anecdotes about a family, pick one of the best and make that your "synopsis" and tell the editor this is your book times one hundred.

The major purpose of the synopsis is to get the reader to want to look at your sample chapters.

Example Synopsis

THE LINE

What if a secret military organization has been covertly manipulating our government's policies for the past fifty years and now appears to be planning a coup?

In 1995 Boomer Watson is a member of the elite Delta Force on a classified mission into the Ukraine when everything goes wrong—the target, instead of radical Ukrainian politicians, turns out to be NATO nuclear inspectors. Returning from the apparently botched mission, Boomer is relieved of his command and sent to Hawaii to get him out of the way. In Hawaii he links up with a former lover and fellow West Pointer, Major Benita Trace, who is working on a novel about an organization she calls THE LINE, referring to the long gray line of West Point graduates.

Working at Fort Shafter, Boomer becomes aware that strange events are occurring. A commander in the 1st Special Forces Group is relieved and a right wing officer takes his place; a covert special operations mission is being planned to coincide with the President's visit to Pearl Harbor on December 7th, a visit where the President will make a speech on his Military Reform Act, which is violently opposed by the military; the Colonel from the office of the Joint Chiefs of Staff who ordered the ill-fated mission in the Ukraine suddenly shows up in Hawaii; a Sergeant Major tells Boomer the story of Boomer's father's death in Vietnam, a story that coincides with Trace's suspicions about The Line.

When Trace's house is broken into and the manuscript is stolen, Boomer begins to take action, going to the north shore of Oahu and observing a classified military operation that isn't supposed to be occurring, while at the same time Trace goes back to the mainland US to talk to the former commander of Special Forces in Vietnam to confirm whether or not The Line exists. Boomer barely escapes with his life and comes to the conclusion that a military coup against the President is planned during a practice commander and control exercise during the President's visit to the Islands.

While Trace meets Rison at the Army-Navy game, Boomer comes into conflict with shadowy military forces on the island of Oahu and in the waters offshore. Just before the SF officer is shot, he gives Trace the location of a diary that holds the key to the Line—the only problem is that to recover it, Trace will have to return to West Point. It becomes a race against time, as December 7th looms closer. The Command and Control exercise is cancelled but it appears that The Line will now attack the President at dawn on the 7th at the Arizona Memorial as he commemorates the 54th anniversary of the Japanese attack.

Not only is the question of the coup to be answered, but further, what is to be done if The Line does indeed exist—an organization that appears to have been responsible for such events as the devastating defeat at Pearl Harbor in 1941; the downing of Gary Power's U-2; the Bay of Pigs; the morass in Vietnam; the debacle of Desert One; and numerous other events. Can the plot be stopped and can such an organization be allowed to exist?

But through the long night of December 6th Boomer learns that what appears to be is and isn't and he is caught in a moral dilemma with a decision to make that will affect the future of the country. For there are more than two sides to this conflict and secrecy and lies surround Boomer and Trace as they try to unravel the truth while at the same time foil the plot against the President. The initial coup that Boomer thought he saw was actually forces moving in to protect the President and the real coup threatens in another direction.

They discover that there is a person on the President's side trying to get the diary for his own purposes and both Boomer and Trace were set up from the very beginning to play their roles in both stopping the coup and recovering the diary.

At the last second, the coup is stopped and the major plotters from The Line are killed. But there is still the loose end of the diary and the person close to the President who got Trace and Boomer involved in the first place without their knowledge. Skibicki kills the President's man and retrieves the diary. In the end, Boomer and Trace go back to

West Point and in an address to the Corps of Cadets, make public the contents, shredding the veil of secrecy all sides wove.

Sample Chapters

Which ones to send? The first two? The last two? The best two? Remember the purpose of the sample chapters. The synopsis gave the reader the story. The chapters are to show the reader how well you write. Some publishers make it easy and tell you to send the first couple. I advise sending consecutive opening chapters. It makes it easier on the reader to stay with the flow of the story. I recommend, even if the publisher doesn't specify, sending the first couple. Sending chapters from the middle or end could be too confusing.

The major purpose of the sample chapters is to get the reader to want to look at your entire manuscript. Do you see the flow here? Cover letter to Synopsis to Sample Chapters to Manuscript.

To justify or not to justify? I justify my format, but my computer spaces evenly. Some programs do not space the words evenly on the line and if yours doesn't, then don't justify.

The title or your name should be on every page along with a page number.

Chapter breaks should start on a new page.

How Quickly Will You Hear Back? From Four Weeks To Never

What's a reasonable amount of time? Whatever the publisher or editor or agent determines it to be.

What can you do if you haven't heard back in what you consider a reasonable amount of time? Nothing. You have no leverage; you can't make people work faster than they are going to.

What will you get back? This will range from nothing, to a "No thanks" written on your cover letter, to a form slip/email thanking you but declining to a personalized letter of rejection. If you get the latter (and they are rare), take some hope. It means someone took the time and effort to actually reply.

Multiple Submissions

Usually it is all right with publishers if you submit to other publishers at the same time. It takes so long for publishers to reply that you'd be a very old person if you did it one at a time. Also remember that December and August are very dead times in the publishing business when most people are on vacation.

I would not bother to put on the cover letter to publishers that it is a multiple submission. It's a subconsciously negative thing and unnecessary. Don't put anything in your cover letter that doesn't serve a positive purpose.

If you do get asked to send in the entire manuscript, it must be in the proper format. I am still amazed that people will spend so much of their time writing, yet the manuscript is not in the correct format. I wonder how people edit a single spaced manuscript?

REJECTIONS

It's not as bad as being betrayed. Et tu Brute.

Why a whole section devoted to rejections? And right after the section on submissions? Because guess what's coming shortly after you start sending out your queries?

Rejection is a fact of life in the writing business and something you *will* face. I have approximately eighty rejections for each of my first two novels. Every publisher my agent sent it to soundly rejected my fourth manuscript. This despite both having an agent representing me and having my first novel out in hardcover. I am currently reworking that manuscript years later using all the comments noted in the rejection letters. My fifth manuscript is gathering dust in my agent's office because we have made a mutual agreement that it is not worth marketing right now and might never be.

A publisher who has done the first six books in a series just rejected me for a seventh book.

If you want to be a writer get used to rejections. It's part of the business.

In fact, the prospect of rejection sometimes keeps writers from sending queries out, which I don't quite understand. If you don't ante up, you can't be in the game.

Ninety percent of the time you will get a form letter thanking you for your query and wishing you luck elsewhere. If you get a personal letter that means someone really took a hard look at what you sent and was interested. Take hope, even though it is a rejection. Read carefully any comments made and take them to heart.

It's essential that you remember that the publishing business is exactly that: A business. Too many writers approach it from an idealistic perspective. The dollar is the bottom line for the publisher. If they don't see how they can make money off your submission—no matter what its literary qualities—then they won't be interested.

Remember that your novel, once it is completed and being submitted is no longer your *baby* but rather a product that you have to distance yourself from emotionally in order for you to survive the ordeal.

I've heard someone once had a Pulitzer Prize winning novel (*The Yearling*) from about thirty years ago typed onto 8.5 by 11 paper and submitted it to a dozen publishing houses. Every single one rejected it. Even if you have an excellent idea and manuscript, you might be rejected simply because they already have a similar manuscript programmed into their production schedule. That has happened to me several times.

There's a book called *Rotten Rejections* edited by Andre Bernard (Pushcart Press, 1990). If you feel bad getting all those form letters, take a peek at this book and be glad you aren't getting some of the personalized rejections others did:

The Bridge Over The River Kwai (Pierre Boulle). A very bad book.

The Good Earth (Pearl Buck). Regret the American public is not interested in anything on China.

The Diary Of Ann Frank (Anne Frank) The girl doesn't, it seems to me, have a special perception or feeling, which would lift that book above the *curiosity* level.

Take heart and hang in there.

Learn to control your emotions with rejection. Sometimes you might get a rejection letter back with comments that you totally disagree with or might be outright incorrect. Don't lash out. The publisher who eventually did publish me initially rejected my first two manuscripts. I was very upset when I got that initial rejection letter back and I disagreed with some of the comments the editor made—but think what might have happened if I had picked up the phone and called him up and chewed him out. Also, after I calmed down, I realized that the comments *were* legitimate.

On a cover letter for a military techno-thriller I sent out, I got back a sentence scrawled in the upper left corner of the letter that read *we don't do fantasies.*

For every acceptance I have (seventeen now) I have at least twenty to thirty rejections on average. I also get rejected for teaching jobs at seminars, magazine articles I submit, etc. etc. It's part of the business and you have to use it to your advantage. Take strength from any positive comment. And also remember that you don't know how and when your break will come—perseverance counts, but you are also dealing with people and courtesy counts also.

Remember that many times the rejection has nothing at all to do with the work itself. There are many reasons for rejection.

Sometimes a publishing house has no room at the inn. Their list is full for the next couple of years and they simply can't buy any more material for a while. Sometimes they don't see how they can market a particular work.

You have to remember who sits at the conference table at a publishing house when they decide whether to buy a manuscript. It's not just the editor who read the manuscript, you also have other editors, the publisher, the marketing people, the sales department, publicity, etc. etc. Sometimes editors may like a work but one of those others sees a problem with it, whether it be not being able to market it, not getting booksellers excited about the type of novel, etc. You have to remember that a publisher has to feel like they can sell the book.

One frustrating aspect of rejections is the second read. The first editor likes your work, but they need a second opinion. So they assign a second editor to look at the manuscript. You have to consider the point of view of this second editor who is looking at something for someone else. Sometimes it will seem to you that everyone can say no, but no one can say yes.

The best advice I received regarding rejection came from an agent at CAA—Creative Artists Agency—when I asked him what the "coverage" was on a manuscript he had sent to a bunch of studios and had rejected. He told me that a rejection is an emotional decision. Then the person who did the rejection goes back and invents reasons for that decision, sometimes correctly, but many times wrongly.

Ask yourself this—why did I buy this book and not that book from the rack in the supermarket last time I was there?

One aspect of rejections I find fascinating is what I call the: "We want something like X, but not like X" theory. I got a rejection back from a studio considering one of my novels and the summary was: "This book is too much like Independence Day and no one wants to be compared to the 4th highest grossing movie of all time." You have to really sit and think about what that sentence says. My reaction is, "Hell, yeah, I want to be compared to such a success."

There's no way around this mindset. In many ways Hollywood and the New York publishing world have 'group-think.' Either everyone wants something or no one wants it. They constantly say they want something different and daring, but they'll reject something because it's different and daring.

The bottom line on rejections is that it is a subjective process.

I recently cut out a newspaper article on a woman who finally had a manuscript accepted. It's her 33rd manuscript—none of the previous ones having been accepted. That's dedication.

There is such a thing as a good rejection if you learn from it and are able to read between the lines. I received a rejection on a new manuscript from an editor who previously bought manuscripts from me at another publishing house. His only comment was: "I like Bob's work, and have bought it before, but this is the same as what he did then."

What I took from that was that I had to get better. I couldn't keep doing the same and expect to move up.

If you do happen to get a 'nasty' rejection where someone makes insensitive comments, console yourself with the thought that you wouldn't want to work with someone who would do such a thing. Remember, if they do it to you, they do it to other people and that is not a formula for success in any business.

You have to have a thick skin as a writer. It's guaranteed, even if you get published, that someone, somewhere, will not like your book, and that at least one of those people will make it their life's mission to inform you of that.

The Agent

Who Are These People And What Do They Do?

The agent is a key player in the traditional publishing business although their role is evolving. If there were no agents, publishing houses would have to hire more people to wade through their slush pile. There are some major publishing houses that won't even look at material if it isn't submitted through an agent. It's simply a question of economics. In fact, in just the past couple of years, that number has grown considerably. There are very few large publishing houses left that will look at unagented material.

The agent is the link between the author and the publishing world. This is most critical for new writers with no background in publishing. It *is* a jungle out there and your agent should be your guide. The agent should know who, where, what, how much, and when.

How To Find An Agent

Most writers hate the quandary that searching for agents put them in. They see the Catch-22 of: I need an agent to get published but I can't get an agent unless I'm published.

That's not really true. Agents are constantly on the lookout for new writers; that's how they stay in business. There are several ways to find an agent.

You can do direct submission using those agents listed in books such as the **Guide To Literary Agents**. Just like publishers, agents list their wants and how to submit to them. There are hundreds listed.

You can get a recommendation from a published author. Remember, though, that this works two ways—the author also should recommend you to the agent. I've had total strangers call me up and ask for the name of my agent and/or editor. Then a few proceed—without asking me—to use my name in a submission saying that I recommended them. Besides being impolite, it really doesn't help. Some people put so much effort (I know because *I* did.) into simply trying to get their work seen, that they tend to overlook the fact that even if it is seen, it might not be worth the look. As I've mentioned in other places, you only have one shot with each person you submit to on each piece of work. Make damn sure it's your best shot.

A thing to remember—it is just as likely that it is the *author's* fault for a bad relationship with an agent as the reverse. Often I hear authors complain bitterly about agents. I always take that with a grain of salt, because ultimately, the person who produces the product is the author, not the agent. If the product is not good, it does not matter how good the agent is. Very rarely will you find an author willing to admit that maybe his writing didn't measure up. Many authors automatically think that if they sold one novel, everything they write from there on out will sell, but actually the facts show the reverse is true.

A book editor that you made a direct submission to might recommend an agent. Remember above where I talked about the role of the agent? An editor who feels your work has some merit, but is not quite up to standard to offer a contract for, might suggest an agent so that you can work with the agent to improve the work. Contrary to popular myth, not all editors enjoy rejecting manuscripts and most of them actually do want to see writers succeed. I should know. I found my agent through an editor who gained nothing at all from the deal (he worked for a non-fiction publisher that in my desperation I had sent my fiction proposal to, which by the way violates the advice an agent just gave out last week at a conference I attended).

Also, many editors prefer negotiating contracts with an agent rather than a new author. They speak the same lingo and have experience. It saves time and aggravation all around. A good agent can negotiate a contract in a matter of minutes because they are familiar with a publisher's boilerplate and know what wiggle room there is.

Instructors at writing seminars can be a good source but like I mentioned above, it works both ways. You should have something that makes them think it's worth their agent's time.

Teachers in MFA programs usually have contacts. This is an old boy/girl network that does take care of its own. If that's the route you take, make the best of it.

I've just gotten on-line and I've noticed some agents advertising through web sites. On-line can be a relatively cheap way to network.

Like most publishers, most agents automatically reject unsolicited manuscripts. However, in a recent copy of *Poets & Writers Magazine* there was a survey that said 227 of 240 agents surveyed would read cold *queries/submissions* received through the mail. I do *not* recommend cold phone calls or faxing queries or e-mailing them. An important point to remember is that if you come off as an irritating person during your contact with the agent, it might not matter how good your manuscript is. The agent simply might not want to work with you. I heard a prominent agent tell of letting go of one of his authors because the author bypassed him and was very rude to some of the people at a publisher.

What About Multiple Submissions To Agents?

My key adjective for the publishing business is SLOW. I said earlier that agents respond quicker than publishers but you could still grow very old waiting. Most agents will only read your work if they have it exclusively. Here's my suggestion:

Do a query to the number one agent on the list you made up from the sources above. Wait a week, and then send to the number two agent. Week three, agent three. Don't tell them it's a multiple query. If an agent calls to ask for the manuscript they will ask you if anyone else has seen the manuscript. Answer honestly. Send the manuscript. Then hold on your submissions to other agents.

The question that always comes up is: What if *another* agent I queried calls and wants to see the manuscript? My reply is: You should be so lucky. But, in the one in a thousand chance you are, tell them it is with the other agent and that you will contact them as soon as you hear back from agent #1. This doesn't necessarily hurt your chances with agent #2, because it actually confirms their interest. Don't try to leverage agent #1 with #2. Have patience, take some sedatives and wait.

How Do I Know If An Agent Is Legitimate?

I am often asked this. My first reply is to use common sense. It's like the person who offers to sell you the Brooklyn Bridge. If an agent promises you they will sell your work, I wouldn't believe them. No agent can make that promise unless they have some sort of kickback deal going with a vanity press.

A legitimate agent should be willing to tell you who some of their clients are and even refer you to one if they want to sign with you.

Remember, though, there is a pecking order to agents. As a new writer, you might not be able to get the number one guy or gal in town. You might hook up with someone who is starting out and has few clients and sales to her name. The bottom line there is to use common sense.

New York State just recently brought charges against an organization that was giving kickbacks to agents who referred clients to it for book doctoring. So there are sharks out there. Be careful. The next chapter is dedicated to this subject.

What Does An Agent Do?

An agent knows the market both in terms of what's selling and who's buying. They also know which houses do which type stories and can direct your manuscript not only to the correct publishers, but also to the correct editors at those publishing houses. They are on top of the latest changes in the publishing industry and should know what the current needs are.

In most contracts, an agent will be the sole source for all literary properties produced by you except if he/she chooses not to take on a work, then it reverts back to you.

Some agents are ex-editors so they have an idea how to make a manuscript marketable. Others spent years working in agencies learning their trade. I was under the mistaken impression that my agent would go through my work with a fine tooth comb, looking over every page carefully. That rarely happens. Again, remember it's a volume business. The same is true of editors to a certain extent. If your manuscript is not basically acceptable in its present form, you won't get a contract. On my first manuscript, my agent faxed me a one page list of suggestions. I made the suggested changes and we eventually sold the manuscript. Ever since then, with every agent I've worked with, they generally tell me in a letter or phone call what their suggestions/problems are with a manuscript and it's up to me to make the corrections.

The key to remember is that if your manuscript is right on the margin of being publishable, it is much more likely that an agent will work with you to make it marketable than an editor will. Editors work with authors under contract and they screen submissions. They very rarely work with something to bring it up to snuff to be offered a contract.

Agents negotiate sale or lease of rights to works, including translation. This includes sales to foreign markets. Normally they charge a higher percentage fee for foreign rights. Most agents have contacts with various foreign representatives and with a Hollywood agent for film rights.

An agent reviews and negotiates contracts. For a new writer who has no idea what the market is like, this is very important. Contracts vary from publisher to publisher and I've seen some terrible ones writers ended up signing. I'll often hear a writer say they'll get a lawyer to review a contract if it comes to that point, but unless they are an entertainment lawyer they won't understand the standards of the business; and entertainment lawyers live in Hollywood and deal with movie people, not books.

Agents collect monies due and render share. This can be very frustrating for both the author and agent, but having the agent do it at least allows the author to maintain a semblance of cordiality with his or her publisher. My rule of thumb is that my agent takes care of all business contacts with my publisher. Once a contract is negotiated, I generally work directly with my editor on the written work unless there is a large difference of opinion.

Agents examine royalty statements (as if anyone could make sense of them to start with.) They are also supposed to check on the publisher's performance and how they handle your manuscript. Just because you are getting published doesn't necessarily mean you are going to make any money. The agent can help you track what the publisher plans on doing with your book, particularly in such important areas as selling the subrights.

Don't expect any paychecks in the mail quickly. Agent Richard Curtis has a running bet with publishers that a writer can write a book faster than they can cut a check. You may laugh, but I have literally done that—written an entire manuscript while waiting for a contract to be drawn up and a check cut.

Like any other business, you have to stay on top of your agent. You are the ultimate protector of your interests. A good agent will advise you, but it should always be your decision as to what actions to take regarding you and your property.

The agent is the business link between you and the publishers. Also remember, though, that the agent ultimately works for himself, not you. Remember, too that the publishers cut the checks, which go to the agent, who takes his/her share and then renders the author his share. So if things start getting sticky between you and your publisher, your agent might not put his or her neck totally on the line to protect your interests simply because they have *other* authors that work with that same publisher and the agent wants to maintain his relationship with the publisher, perhaps to the detriment of your relationship, but this would be a rare case. Ultimately, agents' loyalty lies with their writers rather than the publishers. Also, of course, remember that the reverse is true—your agent holds some power with the editor because the agent might or might not steer future good work toward that publisher depending on the relationship.

Some agents require contracts that stipulate what the roles are and what he/she will do and what you are required to do. Without getting in to too much detail, my main point is that you should work with an agent on a case-by-case basis. What I mean by that is that your agent should have the first chance to look at what you produce. She then should let you know whether she wants to work with you on the manuscript or not. If she doesn't, you are free to do whatever you like with it. This is important because you don't want someone representing you simply because you have a contract—especially if she isn't enthusiastic about a particular manuscript.

To Pay Or Not To Pay?

In many listings, agents are broken down into two categories: those who charge a reading fee and those who don't. You can get varying opinions as to the pros and cons of going to one that charges a reading fee. Take the opinion out and look at the reality of what you want: do you want to get published or do you want feedback on your work? If you want to get published, go to those that don't charge a fee.

I have had no experience with a fee-charging agent so everything I say here is supposition. All I can say about that is that some make their money reviewing manuscripts—not selling them to publishers and getting 15% of what you make. My opinion is don't do it. Try quite a few submissions first. Then if they all come back negative and you get no decent feedback, it's your money. In many cases, it's not necessary to get all 400 pages of your manuscript reviewed. When I look at manuscripts, I can usually tell what problems there are within the first couple of chapters. If you are paying by the page, send a submission (cover letter, one page synopsis, and the first couple of chapters) and see what they say about that, before sending the whole thing.

Make sure you get feedback not only on your manuscript, but also on the synopsis and cover letter.

I would suggest going to writers' conferences and asking around. Sooner or later you will run into someone who has submitted to a fee charging agent and you will get some feedback as to not only the whole process, but about specific agents.

Here is a good example of taking the other person's perspective (which as writers you must be able to do.). How would I operate if I ran an agency that charged a fee for reading submissions? The advantage to me would be I could hire extra people to go through a larger volume of submissions in more detail, searching for those that are deemed publishable (that is also an advantage to you, the writer). Another advantage would be that I might be able to work with someone who is marginal (given that they're paying me some bucks, that is), whereas I wouldn't be able to if my time was my money. Now both of those are true if I was totally honest.

The disadvantage would be that I would tend to focus a lot more energy on making money out of volume of submissions received and be spending a lot of time on un-publishable material (a disadvantage to you the writer). I would also appear to put a lot of time and effort into each submission but in reality I would work off a computer boiler-plate of common mistakes (much like the how-to-write section of this book) and simply go through, make a few changes in the boiler-plate, and send you back thirty pages of apparently in-depth review, which is actually the same as buying a writing book off the shelf at your bookstore except be a lot more expensive. Now these last two are not dishonest but simply a fact of business. I'm not saying that all fee charging agents do either the good or bad. Again, the bottom line is: it's your money.

When is it time to switch agents?

This is an issue almost every published writer runs into sooner or later. I think there are several times:

- You are going nowhere with the agent you have. No sales.
- The agent tells you to go elsewhere.

- You feel like your work is improving but your current agent keeps trying to market it at the same level you've been at. It is an up or out business so this doesn't do you much good.
- You are changing genres and your current agent doesn't like your new genre.
- You want to move up. There are levels to agents just as there are levels to editors. Certain agents can place a manuscript at a certain level in a publishing house. Others can go right to the top.
- Your agents main concern is selling your next book rather than establishing your long term career. The two are not necessarily synonymous.

Ultimately, though, I think it is the same as doing a rewrite on your manuscript. You should feel good after talking to your agent, not bad. You should feel like the agent is representing you in the best possible and *realistic* light. You should feel that your agent views your career as an upward ride.

The bottom line for more writers though is, to be happy if you can get an agent to represent you at all. Remember that agents are business people and are not there to hold your hand or keep you together psychologically while you write (unless of course you write bestsellers.). Also remember that you are not the only client an agent has.

The role of agents is changing as publishing changes. Some agencies are becoming book packagers for authors who are going to self-publish. They provide all the technical services in exchange for a percentage. In essence, they're becoming a form of publisher. They also will market foreign rights and other subrights.

How all this will shake out, remains to be seen.

Writing Groups & Conferences

Networking and realizing you aren't crazy, just peculiar.

We have two shorter books designed specifically for these topics: *The Writers Conference Guide* and *The Critique Group Guide*, but here is some generic information.

Writing tends to be a solitary profession and, as mentioned earlier, one without an apprenticeship program where you can make a living while learning the craft. Writing groups, conferences, and writing programs try to address some of these problems. There are pros and cons to each—things to be gained and things to be lost in participating in any of them, but that mostly depends on what you want.

Writing Groups

These are usually local—several people who enjoy writing band together and start meeting once a month or so. They read to each other and give feedback. Occasionally they bring in different speakers for presentations.

Groups usually have different focuses—short stories, poetry, and novels are the three basic areas. Some groups try to do all areas, with the resultant problem of having to sit through a type of writing that you might not particularly be interested in—but here lies a hidden advantage: as a novelist you just might learn something by listening to poets or short story writers. Not just might—you will, if you have an open mind. You can learn about perspective and you can also learn about the craft of those other mediums. You can also learn about people—not just through the written word but also by observing those who do the writing. I've found that poets, short story writers, novelists, songwriters—all speak some common language, but there are different angles for each area that can add to your repertoire.

I have found, though, that the people who get the least out of the typical writer's group are the novelist. It is very difficult to read a chapter from a novel and get a good critique, especially if you aren't reading the opening chapter. You have to get people up to speed on the story, then have to weather all the "why didn't you..." questions. About one out of ten of those questions are worthwhile. That's not to say as a novelist you shouldn't attend writers' groups and do readings—there are other advantages—it's just to say be aware of the difficulty of reading from a novel in progress at such a group.

I do believe a novelist needs assistance with his or her work. I'm a believer in having friends who are well read and also talking with other writers. As far as a formal group goes it depends if being in the group energizes you or drains you. Also, make sure you aren't in a group where it's a case of the blind leading the blind. Also, are you talking about your book or are you writing it?

An important rule that I believe is necessary for a writers' group (this is also true of writing classes) to survive is: No critiquing of content. Nothing can tear a group apart quicker than people wading into the subject matter—I saw one group run off several writers whose subject matter was religious. The discussion didn't center on the way the person had written the material, but rather became a theological discussion about the material itself. In the same manner, open-mindedness must exist about such things as sex, *profane* language, political views, etc. etc. I think the person who objects to content is the one who has the problem—not the writer. Remember the 1st Amendment.

I was doing a book signing one day and this old lady came up to me and asked me what *language* my books were in. I told her English. She clarified the question by asking me whether I used "profane" language. Since my books were about soldiers, I told her yes, that sort of language fits for those types of characters. She then lectured me that she didn't believe in such language. That's fine for her and anyone else—simply don't buy the book.

However, over the years, I have gotten to the point where for most of my books, I don't use profanity. That's because I get letters from kids every once in a while who read my books. Unless I need it to serve a purpose, I keep it out. Same with sex scenes.

Some writers benefit greatly from critique groups, others not at all. You have to find what works best for you. I am a believer that the best editor for a book is the writer; if the writer is willing to be honest with him or herself.

Conferences And Workshops

These are important. They are the key to networking and publishing is like any other business—who you know is sometimes almost as important as what you do. There is a difference in the way a cold query is treated versus a query an editor or agent can put a face to. You also get to put a face to editors and agents.

One of my pet peeves—, which you probably don't care about anyway, but since I'm writing this book, I get to put down—, is the way conference participants treat editors and agents as if they walk on water and are the source of all valid information. I will spend a week talking about the business of publishing, then they will have a panel of editors and agents on Saturday, and people will ask the same basic questions as if the answers are going to be totally different.

To be honest, that pet peeve stems out of a simple reality of the publishing business—writers are generally at the bottom end of the feeding cycle—especially unpublished writers. Also, just as writers have to pay their dues to earn a place in the business, editors and agents have to do that also. You might feel bad about that rejection slip in your mailbox, but think how that editor who gets a pink slip feels.

A question you should ask yourself when attending a conference is what are the motives of the people who are there. Why are these writers here? I can give you two main reasons—to make some money and to do the same thing you are, network. Usually it's the latter as most conferences only pay enough for the writers to get to the conference, certainly not to make a profit. Writers who are at conferences are there because they like networking also.

Why are these editors here? To look for new writers? Mostly, but I know an editor who has been doing several conferences a year for over a dozen years and has picked up two properties from all that time. To get out of the office? To network with the *other* editors and agents at the conference? To get a free plane ticket and lodging? Whatever. The same is true of agents. I have seen some shysters— fee-charging agents who are there to drum up business. This is not necessarily bad depending on what *you* want. I discussed this topic in the chapter on agents.

One thing to remember is that it is a *writers* conference, not an editor's or agent's conference.

I have quite a bit of respect for people who are willing to take the time and money to attend conferences so that they can learn. My respect goes up even further for those who are willing to truly learn: who are willing to take criticism and suggestions.

Harlan Ellison is well known for eviscerating writers when he holds writing classes. His point is that writing is his profession and those who want to enter it have to be very, very good and he has little patience for those who approach it without the highest standards. In the foreword of one of his novels, Dan Simmons describes attending that class—and being discovered by Harlan Ellison.

I try to be as honest as possible without being rude when working with other writers. Giving false praise wastes everyone's time, but occasionally there are people who do not like hearing anything negative about their project. There are some people who get perturbed that the instructors, editors and agents do not do more to "encourage" the writers. One of the editors responded that that wasn't his job—that was the writers' job.

If you do go to a conference, be prepared. Many have sign-ups where you get to talk to an editor and/or agent for 15 minutes. Have what you are going to say rehearsed. Have your cover letter and one page synopsis in hand. Pitch your idea and story succinctly and in an interesting manner. Don't ever expect to hand the manuscript to them—remember, most are flying home and don't have the space or desire to haul it with them on the plane.

When you get feedback consider it carefully. Don't argue—it won't change their mind about your book, but it will make them think you would be hard to work with.

Use the *free* time constructively. At a conference I recently attended, I sat for two hours in the bar one evening talking with a fellow who had been Bob Hope's top writer for years, picking up information and advice about the business. What amazed me was that all the nights I was there, not a single attendee wandered in and sat down and chatted with the authors, editors and agents who were stuck in the motel. Be willing when the conference director asks for people who want to pick up agents/editors at the airport to volunteer. Take them out to dinner. You might be surprised at what you will reap. I've learned more over a one-hour dinner with editors than sitting for four hours in their lecture during the day.

Treat the people who run the conference with respect and courtesy. They are volunteers who have given tremendously of their time and effort to make sure the conference works. It's not their fault the food the hotel service is bad or that an author or editor missed a meeting.

When you have to make a choice between workshops, my suggestion is to focus more on those given by writers rather than editors and agents. Go to workshops given by people who are where you want to be.

Be prepared. Be able to say what your book is about in one sentence. Be able to say what is unique about your book; what makes it stand out. Don't try to give someone your manuscript; no one is going to lug it home. When asking questions in a workshop or panel, try to make them generic rather than "I've just written a book about x, y, and z, and I want to know . . . ."

Sell yourself if you have something to sell. For example, I once worked with a writer whose husband had been a Formula One race car driver and she was writing a thriller based in that world. She had something to talk about that most people knew little about.

Do people actually get *discovered* at conferences? Yes. I just received an e-mail from a successful writer who told me how he got his first book contract set up at a conference. A few months ago a man who was in my group at the Maui Writers Retreat e-mailed me to tell me of his two book deal.

I'm getting toward the close of this book and this issue of conferences brings up something that dovetails into what I've written on all these pages. I recently listened to an agent talk about mid-career writers and the mistakes they make. The next morning I saw him at breakfast and sat down with him and told him that what he had said the previous day had really struck home. The interesting thing, I continued, was that if I had heard what he'd said a year previously, I would have understood it intellectually but I wouldn't have accepted it emotionally.

I think that is a critical aspect of being a writer. Much of what I've written in this book you might have nodded at and said to yourself "well, that's common sense." But do you really believe it? There is a gap between understanding and acceptance. That gap can cause not just writers, but anyone, great trouble in their life. I've noted that my current agent never really confronts me with anything. Also, he sometimes won't give me advice when I ask for it. I've realized it's not because he's bored or doesn't have time, but rather, like a good psychologist, he can point me in the right direction, but he knows that whether I decide to go there or not is totally up to me. In fact, if he did give me advice I wasn't ready to hear, I could end up reacting and going totally in the wrong direction.

Things I wrote in this book five years ago I've since cut out and replaced with words that are the exact opposite. Yet I believed what I had written five years ago just as much as I believe what I am writing now. What happened? Through experience and some open-mindedness, I learned that I needed to change the way I viewed things.

How to find a conference? The Writers Market has a listing. Also, on the Internet, you can go to Shawguides at: http://writing.shawguides. com/

In Closing

Quite a bit of what you just read won't make very much sense–or too much sense—to you if you are just beginning to write manuscripts. But reread it every once in a while and you will find that the more you write, the more sense it makes. I read numerous writing books when I first began and got quite frustrated because a lot of it seemed very simple or I didn't agree with some of the things that were said. But I didn't truly understand until I tried writing. Then it all begins clicking into place.

Remember—writing is work. You must put the time and effort into it to succeed.

So, although I said there is no right or wrong, I will leave you with one simple rule:

WRITE.

Then.

WRITE SOME MORE.

Then. Yep. WRITE EVEN MORE.

Non-Fiction By Bob Mayer

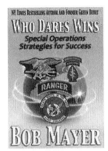

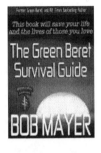

Books By Bob Mayer And Jen Talty

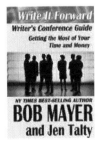

Other Books By Bob Mayer

"Thelma and Louise go clandestine." *Kirkus Reviews on Bodyguard of Lies*

" . . .delivers top-notch action and adventure, creating a full cast of lethal operatives armed with all the latest weaponry. Excellent writing and well-drawn, appealing characters help make this another taut, crackling read." *Publishers Weekly*

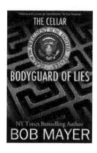

"Fascinating, imaginative and nerve-wracking." *Kirkus Reviews*

The Presidential Series By Bob Mayer

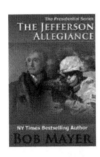

Coming 5 November

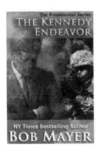

The Green Beret Series

"Mayer has stretched the limits of the military action novel. Synbat is also a gripping detective story and an intriguing science fiction thriller. Mayer brings an accurate and meticulous depiction of military to this book which greatly enhances its credibility." *Assembly*

"Will leave you spellbound. Mayer's long suit is detail, giving the reader an in-depth view of the inner workings of the Green Machine." *Book News*

"Mayer keeps story and characters firmly under control. The venal motives of the scientists and military bureaucracy are tellingly contrasted with the idealism of the soldiers. A treat for military fiction readers." *Publishers Weekly*

"Sinewy writing enhances this already potent action fix. An adrenaline cocktail from start to finish." *Kirkus Reviews*

Historical Fiction By Bob Mayer

Shadow Warrior Series

"Sizzling, first rate war fiction." *Library Journal*

"A military thriller in the tradition of John Grisham's The Firm." *Publishers Weekly*

"The Omega Missile comes screaming down on target. A great action read." *Stephen Coonts*

"What a delicious adventure-thriller. Its clever, plausible plot gives birth to lots of action and suspense." *Kansas City Journal Inquirer*

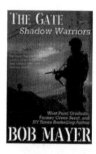

The Atlantis Series By Bob Mayer

"Spell-binding! Will keep you on the edge of your seat. Call it techno-thriller, call it science fiction, call it just terrific story-telling." *Terry Brooks, #1 NY Times Bestselling author of the Shannara series and Star Wars Phantom Menace*

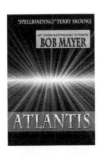

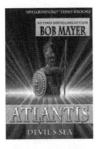

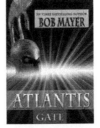

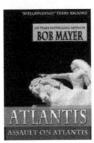

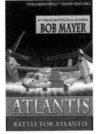

Psychic Warrior Series

"A pulsing technothriller. A nailbiter in the best tradition of adventure fiction." *Publishers Weekly.*

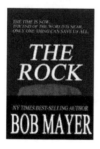

Area 51/Nightstalkers Series

"Bob Mayer's *Nightstalkers* grabs you by the rocket launcher and doesn't let go. Fast-moving military SF action—just the way I like it. Highly recommend." *B.V. Larson*

About Bob Mayer

NY Times bestselling author **Bob Mayer** has had over 50 books published. He has sold over four million books, and is in demand as a team-building, life-changing, and leadership speaker and consultant for his *Who Dares Wins: The Green Beret Way* concept, which he translated into Write It Forward: a holistic program teaching writers how to be authors. He is also the Co-Creator of Who Dares Wins Publishing, which does both eBooks and Print On Demand, so he has experience in both traditional and non-traditional publishing.

His books have hit the *NY Times*, *Publishers Weekly*, *Wall Street Journal* and numerous other bestseller lists. His book *The Jefferson Allegiance,* was released independently and reached #2 overall in sales on Nook.

Bob Mayer grew up in the Bronx. After high school, he entered West Point where he learned about the history of our military and our country. During his four years at the Academy and later in the Infantry, Mayer questioned the idea of "mission over men." When he volunteered and passed selection for the Special Forces as a Green Beret, he felt more at ease where the men were more important than the mission.

Mayer's obsession with mythology and his vast knowledge of the military and Special Forces, mixed with his strong desire to learn from history, is the foundation for his science fiction series *Atlantis, Area 51* and *Psychic Warrior*. Mayer is a master at blending elements of truth into all of his thrillers, leaving the reader questioning what is real and what isn't.

He took this same passion and created thrillers based in fact and riddled with possibilities. His unique background in the Special Forces gives the reader a sense of authenticity and creates a reality that makes the reader wonder where fact ends and fiction begins.

In his historical fiction novels, Mayer blends actual events with fictional characters. He doesn't change history, but instead changes how history came into being.

Mayer's military background, coupled with his deep desire to understand the past and how it affects our future, gives his writing a rich flavor not to be missed.

Bob has presented for over a thousand organizations both in the United States and internationally, including keynote presentations, all day workshops, and multi-day seminars. He has taught organizations ranging from Maui Writers, to Whidbey Island Writers, to San Diego State University, to the University of Georgia, to the Romance Writers of America National Convention, to Boston SWAT, the CIA, Fortune-500, the Royal Danish Navy Frogman Corps, Microsoft, Rotary, IT Teams in Silicon Valley and many others. He has also served as a Visiting Writer for NILA MFA program in Creative Writing. He has done interviews for the *Wall Street Journal*, *Forbes*, *Sports Illustrated*, PBS, NPR, the Discovery Channel, the SyFy channel and local cable shows. For more information see www.bobmayer.org.

Made in the USA
Middletown, DE
26 June 2016